SPOTLIGHT on MUSIC™

Authors

Judy Bond

René Boyer

Margaret Campbelle-Holman

Emily Crocker

Marilyn C. Davidson

Robert de Frece

Virginia Ebinger

Mary Goetze

Betsy M. Henderson

John Jacobson

Michael Jothen

Chris Judah-Lauder

Carol King

Vincent P. Lawrence

Ellen McCullough-Brabson

Janet McMillion

Nancy L. T. Miller

Ivy Rawlins

Susan Snyder

Gilberto D. Soto

Kodály Contributing Consultant

Sr. Lorna Zemke

HAL•LEONARD®

MACMILLAN McGRAW-HILL

i

ACKNOWLEDGMENTS

Creative Direction and Delivery: The Quarasan Group, Inc.

From the Top-On National Radio! student features are adapted from the nationally distributed public radio program, *From the Top.* CEOs/Executive Producers: Jennifer Hurley-Wales and Gerald Slavet. Authors: Ann Gregg and Joanne Robinson. © 2001, 2002, 2003 From the Top, Inc.

The Broadway Junior® logo and MTI® logo are trademarks of Music Theatre International. All rights reserved.

Grateful acknowledgment is given to the following authors, composers and publishers. Every effort has been made to trace the ownership of all copyrighted material and to secure the necessary permissions to reprint these selections. In the case of some selections for which acknowledgment is not given, extensive research has failed to locate the copyright holders.

Addams Family Theme, The, Music and Lyrics by Vic Mizzy. Copyright © 1964, Renewed 1992 by Unison Music Company. Administered by Next Decade Entertainment, Inc. International Copyright Secured. All Rights Reserved.

Ballad of the Bedbugs and the Beetles, traditional. Reprinted in *Ready-to-Use Activities for Before and After School Programs,* by Verna Stassevitch, Patricia Stemmler, Rita Shotwell, and Marian Wirth. The Center for Applied Research in Education, Copyright © 1998. Music by Carol King. All Rights Reserved. Used by Permission.

Bohm (Spring Has Come!), Words by Chu Shik Ham, Music by Sou Chul Chang. Copyright © by SEH KWANG PUBLISHING CO. International Copyright Secured. All Rights Reserved.

Boo!, Words and Music by Cheryl Lavender. Copyright © 2002 by HAL LEONARD CORPORATION. International Copyright Secured. All Rights Reserved.

Chag Asif (Harvest Time), Original Words and Music by Sarah Levy-Tanai, English Words by Laura Koulish. Original Words and Music Copyright © by Levy-Tanai & Rappaport Moshe, Israel. English Words Copyright © Laura Koulish. International Copyright Secured. All Rights Reserved. Reprinted by Permission of ACUM, Ltd.

City Life (with I Love the Mountains), Words and Music by John Jacobson and Alan Billingsley. Copyright © 2000 by HAL LEONARD CORPORATION. International Copyright Secured. All Rights Reserved.

Colors of the Wind, Music by Alan Menken. Lyrics by Stephen Schwartz. From Walt Disney's POCAHONTAS. Copyright © 1995 Wonderland Music Company, Inc.. and Walt Disney Music Company. All Rights Reserved. Used by Permission.

Consider Yourself, Words and Music by Lionel Bart. Copyright © 1960 (Renewed). Lakeview Music Co. Ltd., London, England. TRO - Hollis Music, Inc., New York, controls all publication rights for the U.S.A. and Canada. International Copyright Secured. All Rights Reserved Including Public Performance For Profit. Used by Permission.

Deep in the Heart of Texas, Words by June Hershey. Music by Don Swander. Copyright © 1941 by Melody Lane Publications, Inc. Copyright Renewed. International Copyright Secured. All Rights Reserved.

Digga Digga Dog, from Walt Disney Pictures' 102 DALMATIANS. Words and Music by Pamela Phillips Oland, Mark Brymer, George Clinton, Jr., Garry M. Shider and David L. Spradley. Copyright © 2000 Walt Disney Music Company, Bridgeport Music, Inc., and Southfield Music, Inc. All Rights Reserved. Used by Permission. Contains sampling of "Atomic Dog" by George Clinton.

Ding Dong Diggy Diggy Dong, Words and Music by Carl Orff. Copyright © 1958 by Schott & Co. c/o European American Music. International Copyright Secured. All Rights Reserved.

Eight Days of Hanukkah, The, Words and Music by George David Weiss. Copyright © 1987 by ABILENE MUSIC, INC. c/o THE SONGWRITERS GUILD OF AMERICA. All Rights Reserved.

El atole (The Atole), Mexican Folk Song. Adapted by Jose-Luis Orozco. Copyright © 1987 by Jose-Luis Orozco/Arcoiris Records, P.O. Box 461900, Los Angeles, CA 90046. International Copyright Secured. All Rights Reserved.

Evergreen, Everblue, Words and Music by Raffi Cavourkian. Copyright © by Homeland Publishing, a div. of Troubadour Music, Inc. International Copyright Secured. All Rights Reserved.

Flip, Flop and Fly, Words and Music by Charles Calhoun and Lou Willie Turner. Copyright © 1955 by Unichappell Music Inc. Copyright Renewed. International Copyright Secured. All Rights Reserved.

Frosty the Snow Man, Words and Music by Steve Nelson and Jack Rollins. Copyright © 1950 by Chappell & Co. Copyright Renewed. International Copyright Secured. All Rights Reserved.

Greatest Show on Earth, The. from the Paramount Motion Picture THE GREATEST SHOW ON EARTH. Words by Ned Washington. Music by Victor Young. Copyright © 1952 (Renewed 1981) by Famous Music Corporation. International Copyright Secured. All Rights Reserved.

Happy Wanderer, The, Words by Antonia Ridge. Music by Friedrich W. Moller. Copyright © 1954 and 1982 by Bosworth & Co., Ltd., London for all countries. All Rights for the United States of America and Canada assigned to Sam Fox Publishing Company, Inc., Santa Barbara, California. International Copyright Secured. All Rights Reserved.

I Walk in Beauty, Words and Music by Arliene Nofchissey. Copyright © Laminite Publishers. International Copyright Secured. All Rights Reserved.

I'm a Believer, Words and Music by Neil Diamond. Copyright © 1966. Renewed 1978. STONEBRIDGE MUSIC and FORAY MUSIC. All Rights Reserved. International Copyright Secured. Used by Permission.

Interjections, From MTI's Broadway Junior Broadway for Kids SCHOOLHOUSE ROCK LIVE! Junior. Music and Lyrics by Lynn Ahrens. Copyright © Music and Lyrics 1995 and TM American Broadcasting Companies, Inc. The above copyright notice may be subject to conform to new or different requirements upon written notification from American Broadcasting Companies, Inc. All Rights Reserved. Used by Permission.

Interplanet Janet, From MTI's Broadway Junior Broadway for Kids SCHOOLHOUSE ROCK LIVE! Junior. Music and Lyrics by Lynn Ahrens. Copyright © Music and Lyrics 1995 and TM American Broadcasting Companies, Inc. The above copyright notice may be subject to change to conform to new or different requirements upon written notification from American Broadcasting Companies, Inc. All Rights Reserved. Used by Permission.

It's Time to Get Ready for Christmas, Words and Music by Emily Crocker and John Higgins. Copyright © 1992 by Jenson Publications. International Copyright Secured. All Rights Reserved.

Jamaica Farewell, Words and Music by Irving Burgie. Copyright © 1955. Renewed 1983. Cherry Lane Music Publishing Company, Inc. (ASCAP). Lord Burgess Music Publishing Company (ASCAP) and DreamWorks Songs (ASCAP). Worldwide Rights for Lord Burgess Music Publishing Company and DreamWorks Songs Administered by Cherry Lane Music Publishing Company, Inc. International Copyright Secured. All Rights Reserved.

Just Like the Sun, Words and Music by Raffi Cavourkian. Copyright © by Homeland Publishing, a div. of Troubadour Music, Inc. International Copyright Secured. All Rights Reserved.

La mar (The Sea), Mexican Folk Song, English Lyrics and Arrangement by Jose-Luis Orozco. Copyright © by Arcoiris Records, Inc. International Copyright Secured. All Rights Reserved.

Limbo Rock, Words and Music by Billy Strange and Jon Sheldon. Copyright © 1961 Sony/ATV Songs LLC. Copyright Renewed. All Rights Administered by Sony/ATV Music Publishing, 8 Music Square West, Nashville, TN 37203. International Copyright Secured. All Rights Reserved.

continued on page 409

The McGraw·Hill Companies

Published by Macmillan/McGraw-Hill, of McGraw-Hill Education, a division of The McGraw-Hill Companies, Inc., Two Penn Plaza, New York, New York 10121.

Printed in the United States of America
ISBN 0-02-295901-7 / 3
5 6 7 8 9 071/043 10 09 08 07 06 05

CONTRIBUTORS

Consultants

Brian Burnett,
Movement

Stephen Gabriel,
Technology

Magali Iglesias,
English Language Learners

Roberta Newcomer,
Special Learners/Assessment

Frank Rodríguez,
English Language Learners

Jacque Schrader,
Movement

Kathy B. Sorensen,
International Phonetic
Alphabet

Patti Windes-Bridges,
Listening Maps

Linda Worsley,
Listening/Singable
English Translations

Sr. Lorna Zemke,
Kodály Contributing
Consultant

Contributing Writers

Allison Abucewicz
Sharon Berndt
Rhona Brink
Ann Burbridge
Debbie Helm Daniel
Katherine Domingo
Kari Gilbertson
Janet Graham
Hilree Hamilton
Linda Harley
Judy Henneberger
Carol Huffman
Bernie Hynson, Jr.
Sheila A. Kerley
Ellen Mendelsohn

Cristi Cary Miller
Leigh Ann Mock
Patricia O'Rourke
Barbara Resch
Isabel Romero
Carl B. Schmidt
Debra Shearer
Ellen Mundy Shuler
Carol Wheeler
Sheila Woodward

Recordings

Executive Producer
John Higgins

Senior Music Editor/Producer
Emily Crocker

Senior Recording Producer
Mark Brymer

Recording Producers
Steve Millikan
Andy Waterman

Associate Recording Producers
Alan Billingsley, Darrell
Bledsoe, Stacy Carson,
Emily Crocker, Rosanna

Eckert, John Egan,
Chad Evans, Darlene
Koldenhoven,
Chris Koszuta, Don
Markese, Matthew
McGregor, Steve Potts,
Edwin Schupman, Michael
Spresser, Frank Stegall,
David Vartanian, Mike
Wilson, Ted Wilson

Project/Mastering Engineer
Mark Aspinall

Post Production Engineer
Don Sternecker

Multicultural Consultants

William Anderson, Chet-Yeng Loong, Edwin Schupman, Kathy B.
Sorensen, Gilberto D. Soto, Judith Cook Tucker, Dennis Waring

In the Spotlight Consultant

Willa Dunlevy

Multicultural Advisors

Brad Ahawanrathe Bonaparte (Mohawk), Emmanuel Akakpo (Ewe), Earlene Albano (Hawaiian), Luana Au (Maori), Ruby Beeston (Mandarin), Latif Bolat (Turkey), Estella Christensen (Spanish), Oussama Davis (Arabic), Mia Delguardo (Minahasa), Nolutho Ndengane Diko (Xhosa), Angela Fields (Hopi, Chemehuevi), Gary Fields (Lakota, Cree), Gilad Harel (Hebrew), Josephine Hetarihon (Bahasa Indonesian, Minahasa, and Maluko dialect), Judy Hirt-Manheimer (Hebrew), Rose Jakub (Navajo), Elizabeth Jarema (Fijian), Rita Jensen (Swedish), Malou Jewett (Visayan), Alejandro Jimenez (Hispanic), Chris Jones (Hungarian), Wendy Jyang Shamo (Mandarin), Amir Kalay (Hebrew), Michael Katsan (Greek), Silvi Madarajan (Tamil), Georgia Magpie (Comanche), Nona Mardi (Malay), Aida Mattingly (Tagalog), Mike Kanathohare McDonald (Mohawk), Vasana de Mel (Sinhala), Marion Miller (Czech), Etsuko Miskin (Japanese), Mogens Mogenson (Danish), Kenny Tahawisoren Perkins (Mohawk), Pradeep Nayyar (Punjabi, Hindi), Renu Nayyar (Punjabi), Mfanego Ngwenya (Zulu), Wil Numkena (Hopi), Samuel Owuru (Akan), Nina Padukone (Konkani), Hung Yong Park (Korean), James Parker (Finnish), Jose Pereira (Konkani), Berrit Price (Norwegian), John Rainer (Taos Pueblo, Creek), Lillian Rainer (Taos Pueblo, Creek, Apache), Arnold Richardson (Haliwa-Saponi), Ken Runnacles (German), Trudy Shenk (German), Ron Singer (Navajo), Ernest Sive (Cahuilla, Serrano [Maringa']), Bonnie Slade (Swedish), Cristina Sorrentino (Portuguese), Diane Thram (Xhosa), Elena Todorov (Bulgarian), Zlatina Todorov (Russian), Tom Toronto (Lao, Thai), Rebecca Wilberg (French, Italian), Sheila Woodward (Zulu), Keith Yackeyonny (Comanche)

Contents

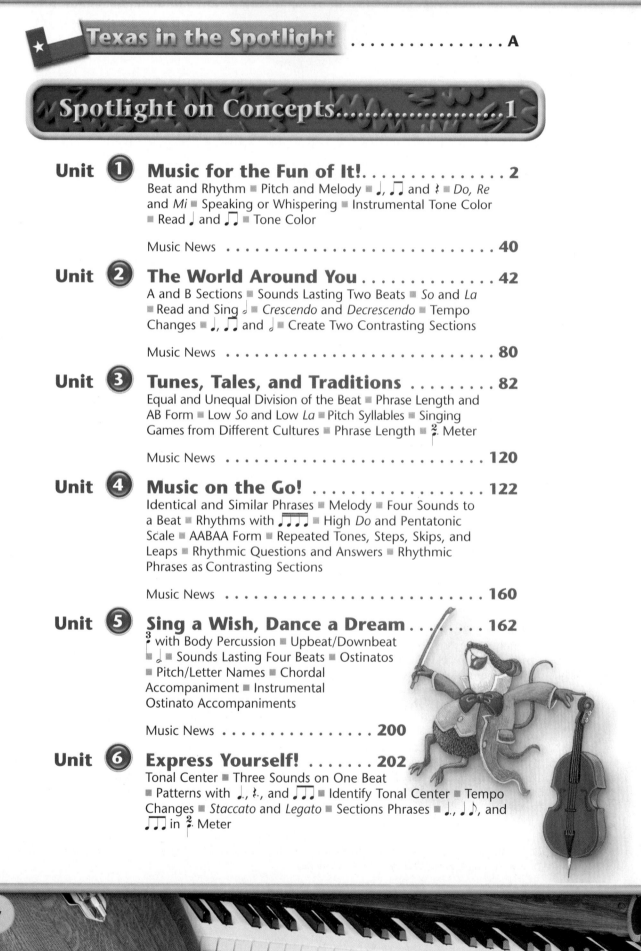

Spotlight on Music Reading..........241

Spotlight on Performance............289

Texas

Turn the spotlight on Texas.
See the dancers dancing
the Cotton-Eye Joe.
Hear the singers singing jazz and blues,
boleros and rock and roll.
Listen to the music:
tejano, norteño, zydeco,
mariachi, and more.
Watch artists paint pictures
of the hills and valleys,
rivers and streams
of this great state.
Read about Spanish missions
and revolutions,
astronauts and cowboys,
outlaws and heroes.
When you turn the spotlight on Texas,
you can see the Lone Star shine!

I'm from
Texas, too!

Van Cliburn, ▶
classical pianist

in the Spotlight

◀ Stevie Ray Vaughan, blues guitarist and singer

Ornette ▶ Coleman, jazz saxophone player

▼ Mariachi band and dancers

B

The music of Texas shines like the stars!
When I sing alone, I light up the room.
When we sing together,
we light up the sky!

step into the Spotlight

**Spotlight CD
Track 1**

Words and Music by John Jacobson,
Emily Crocker, and John Higgins

1. Lis - ten to the world a - round you, There is
2. In a world of sound and col - or, in a

mu - sic ev - 'ry - where.__ Just step out - side__ your
rhy - thm all its own,____ It's the heart - beat of__ our

door - way, and you can hear mu - sic in the air!__
Tex - as, the land we proud - ly call our home!_

From the cit - y to the farm and field,__ to the
From the cit - y to the farm and field,__ there's a

The Texas star shines on plants and animals.
It shines on special things such as the state seal and the state flag.

The Texas Seal

The Texas Flag

The Texas Stone: Palmwood

The Texas Bird: Mockingbird

The Texas Insect: Monarch Butterfly

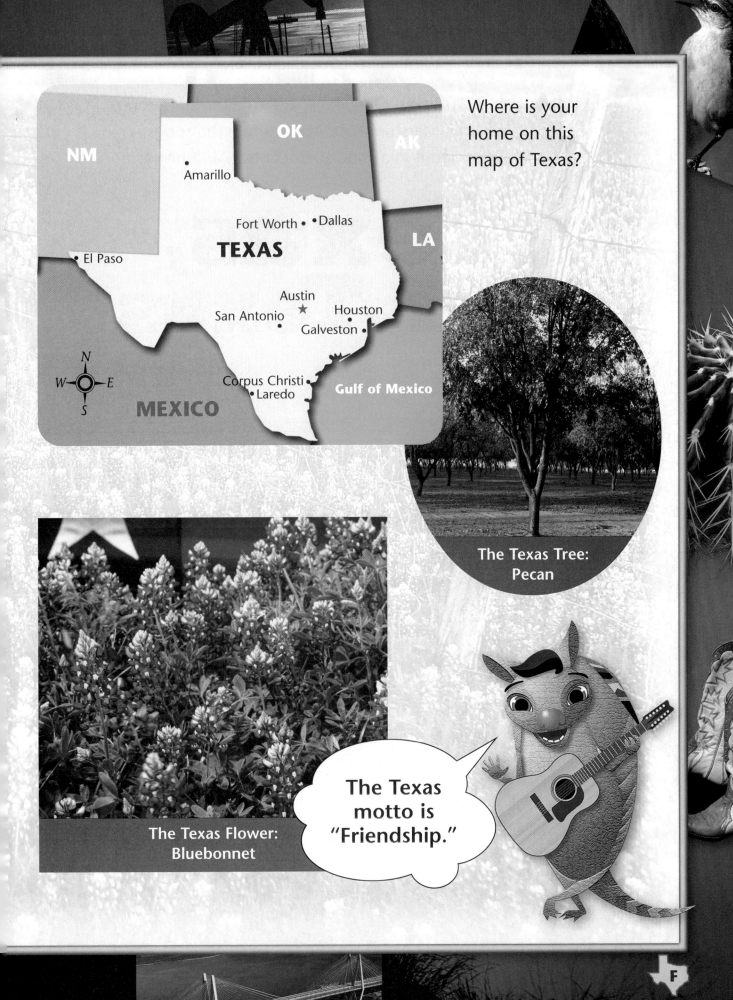

Where is your home on this map of Texas?

NM

OK

AK

· Amarillo

Fort Worth · · Dallas

TEXAS

· El Paso

LA

Austin
San Antonio ★   Houston
· Galveston ·

N
W—E
S

Corpus Christi ·
· Laredo   **Gulf of Mexico**

MEXICO

The Texas Tree:
Pecan

The Texas Flower:
Bluebonnet

The Texas
motto is
"Friendship."

In 1929 "Texas, Our Texas" became the state song.
William J. Marsh of Fort Worth wrote the song.
He entered it in a state song contest, and he won!

Texas, Our Texas

Spotlight CD
Track 4
Verse

Words by Gladys Yoakum Wright
and William J. Marsh
Music by William J. Marsh

1. Tex - as, our Tex - as! all hail the might - y State!
2. Tex - as, our Tex - as! Your free-born Sin - gle Star,
3. Tex - as, our Tex - as! From ty - rant grip now free,

Tex - as, our Tex - as! So won - der - ful, so great.
Sends out its ra - diance To na - tions near and far,
Shines forth in splen-dor, Your Star of Des - ti - ny!

Bold - est and grand-est, With - stand - ing ev - 'ry test; O
Em - blem of Free-dom, It sets our hearts a - glow, With
Mo - ther of He - roes, We come your chil - dren true, Pro -

Em - pire wide and glo - rious, You stand su - preme - ly blest.
thoughts of San Ja - cin - to And glo - rious Al - a - mo.
claim-ing our al - le - giance, Our Faith, Our Love for you.

Every day we pledge our allegiance to the United States of America and to our state!

Here is the Texas pledge.

Honor the Texas flag:
I pledge allegiance
to thee, Texas,
one and indivisible.

Refrain

God bless you Tex - as! And keep you brave and strong, That

(repeat refrain)

you may grow in pow'r and worth, Through-out the ag - es long.

There's a star that shines in Texas!
It's been there for thousands of years.
For thousands of years, the brightest stars
have always been the Texans themselves.
There's a star that shines in Texas, no matter
how things change.

◀ Oilwell in
Beaumont

Chuck ▶
wagon

▼ The Alamo

▼ Stetson hat

▼ Davy Crockett

▼ Lady Bird Johnson

Francisco Vasquez ▶
de Coronado,
Spanish explorer

We've had two United States Presidents born in Texas!

Dwight D.
Eisenhower

Lyndon B.
Johnson

A Texas Classic

When a cowboy sleeps, he dreams of the open range.

His dreams are filled with wide-open spaces.

His heart is full of freedom.

When the cowboy wakes, he sings the songs that match his dreams.

Don't Fence Me In

Spotlight CD
Track 7

Words and Music by Cole Porter

Oh, give me land, lots of land un-der star-ry skies a-bove.

don't fence me in.____ Let me ride through the wide o-pen

coun-try that I love, don't fence me in. Let me

be by my-self in the eve-ning breeze, lis-ten to the mur-mur of the

cot-ton-wood trees.__ Send me off for-ev-er but I ask you please,

The Texas star shines in the history and culture
of people whose families came from Spain,
Mexico, Central America, or South America.
We celebrate our Hispanic heritage!
It's like a star that shines ...

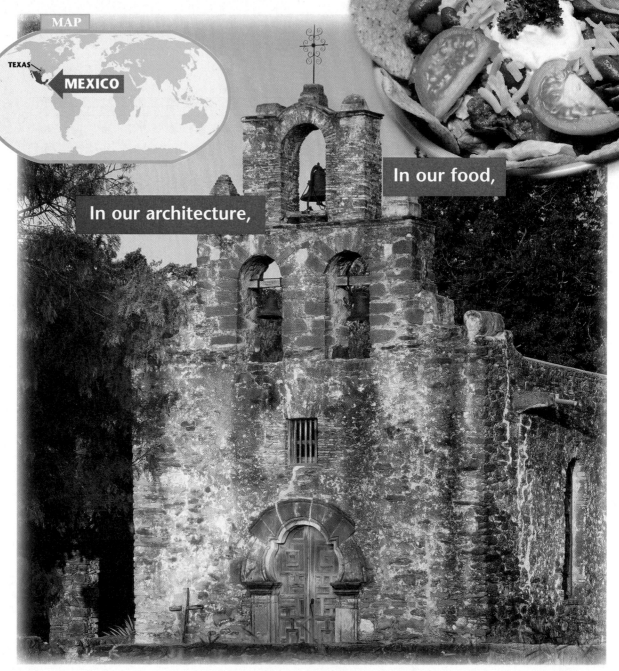

MAP

TEXAS

MEXICO

In our architecture,

In our food,

▲ Mission San Francisco de la Espada

In our language,

Viva Texas!

And especially in our music!

A Texas Star!

Amado Peña is an artist. He was born in Laredo in 1943. In his art he shows the beauty of the Southwest and tells stories about his people. He attended Texas A&I University (now called Texas A&M—Kingsville.) For 16 years he taught art in Texas schools. He still does what he can to give students in Texas, New Mexico, Arizona, and Colorado a chance to study the arts.

Music Mexican Style

Texas is a land of music!
Much of that music comes from our Hispanic heritage:
mariachi, norteño, tejano, conjunto, ranchero.
Texas is a land of music!

El Reino del Revés

The Land of Upside-Down

Spotlight CD
Track 10

Words and Music by Maria Elena Walsh
English Lyrics by MMH

Verse

D7   G   C

Spanish: 1. Me di - je - ron que en el Rei - no del Re - vés na - da el
Pronunciation: me ði xe ɾon ken el ɾei no ðel ɾe βes na ðel
English: 1. In the land of up - side down all the

D7   G   D7

pá - ja - ro y vue - la el pez, que los
pɑ xa ɾo i βwe la el pes ke los
birds swim and fish - es fly. And the

G   C

ga - tos no ha - cen miau y di - cen "yes" por - que es -
ɡa tos noa sen myau i ði sen poɾ kes
cats don't me - ow, they say "hel - lo" and I

D7   G

tu - di - an mu - cho in - glés.
tu ði an mu cho in gles
real - ly don't un - der - stand why.

◀ Valerio Longoria, Sr.,
conjunto accordianist

▲ Mariachi band

Refrain

Va-mos a ver co-mo es el Rei - no del Re - vés___
ba mos a βer ko mo es el rei no ðel re βes

Va-mos a ver co-mo es el Rei - no del Re - vés___
ba mos a βer ko mo es el rei no ðel re βes

2. Me dijeron que en el Reino del Revés
   cabe un oso en una nuez,
   que usan barbas y bigotes los bebés
   y que un año dura un mes.

   me ðixeron ken el reino ðel reβes
   kabe un oso en una nwes
   keu san barbas i bigotes los βeβes
   i keun anyo ðura un mes

2. In the land of upside down
   Señor bear fits in a glass.
   All the babies wear mustaches
   and a year just one month lasts.

Big Cities, Small Towns

Texas is a state of variety.
There are plains and mountains,
deserts and lush green valleys.
There are beaches and forests,
lowlands and highlands.
There are farms and ranches,
orchards and prairies.
In Texas, there are wet regions
and dry regions,
hot and cold and in between.
Whether you live in a big city
or in a tiny little town,
if your home is in Texas,
you're in the right place!

▲ Lubbock

◀ San Antonio

▼ Austin

Texas Is Good Natured!

◀ Albany

▲ Great Horned Owl

▲ Javelina

▲ McKinney

◀ Turkey Vulture

That's one funny looking pig!

R

Shine the spotlight on Texas!
Let us sing the songs.
Let us tell the stories.
Let us dance the dances and play the tunes.
Shine the spotlight on Texas and let us shine!
Shine! Shine!

**Spotlight CD
Track 14**

The Yellow Rose of Texas
Traditional Folk Song
Deep in the Heart of Texas
Words by June Hershey
Music by Don Swandor

1. There's a yel - low rose in Tex - as, I'm
(2.) sweet - est lit - tle rose - bud that

go - ing there to see, No oth - er fel - low
Tex - as ev - er knew. Her eyes are bright as

knows her, no - bod - y else but me. She
dia - monds, they spark - le like the dew. You can

cried so when I left her, it al - most broke my
talk a - bout your dear ones and sing of Ro - sa

Ella, Bisonte y la Tierra

Amado M. Peña, Jr. (b. 1943), showed a talent for art when he was a boy, and he has been painting for many years. After a trip to southern Mexico, he began painting pictures that show the mixture of his Mexican and Native American heritage. He puts into his art what he sees around him and what he sees inside himself. He believes that art begins with the heart and soul of the people.

heart, and if we ev - er meet a - gain we
Lee, but the yel - low rose of Tex - as is the

nev - er more shall part. 2. She's the
on - ly one for

me.

1. The stars at
2. The sage in

Van Cliburn (b. 1934) is a pianist who lives in Fort Worth, Texas. He began to study piano with his mother when he was three. At the age of twelve, he played a concert with the Houston Symphony Orchestra. In 1958 he won the First International Tchaikovsky Competition in Moscow. His talent made people around the world interested in classical music. In 1962 he began the Van Cliburn International Piano Competition, held in Fort Worth every four years.

Celebrate Texas!

Let's celebrate Texas
and all that makes it shine!
Celebrate the music, the flowers,
and the animals.
Celebrate the heroes of today
and yesterday.
Celebrate all that makes us alike
and all that makes us different.
Celebrate Texas, for Texas is us,
and we're what makes Texas great!

▼ Conjunto musician

Livestock ▶
Show Parade

Wahoo!

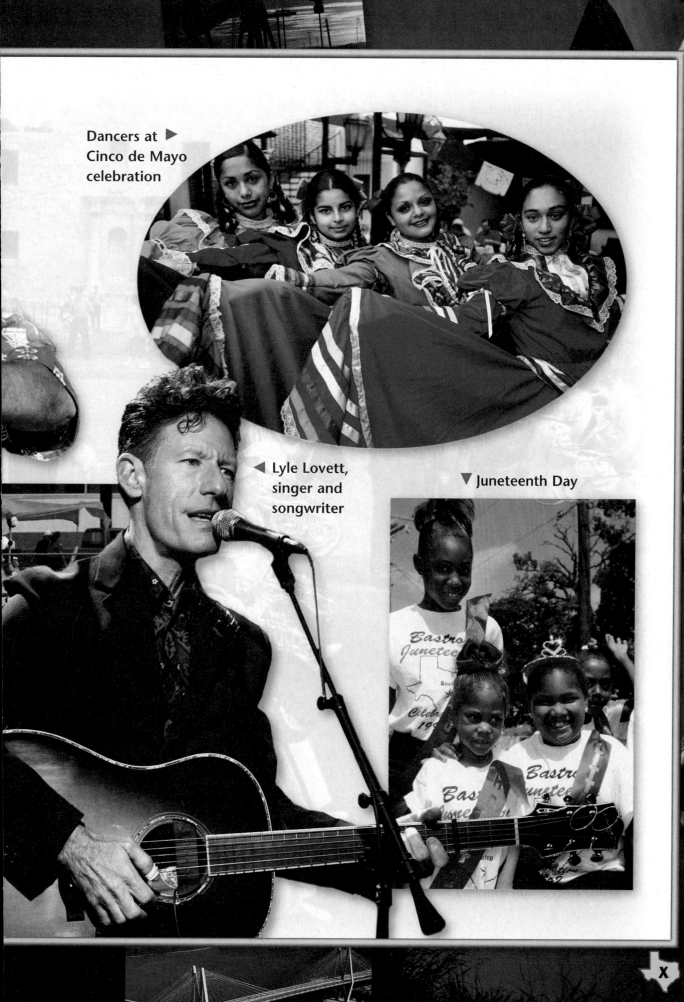

Dancers at ▶
Cinco de Mayo
celebration

◀ Lyle Lovett,
singer and
songwriter

▼ Juneteenth Day

Spotlight on
Concepts

Spotlight on Concepts

Spotlight on Concepts

Music for the Fun of It!

Music makes sharing and playing more fun. Music can bring fun to many things you do. Look at the picture. How are these children sharing through music?

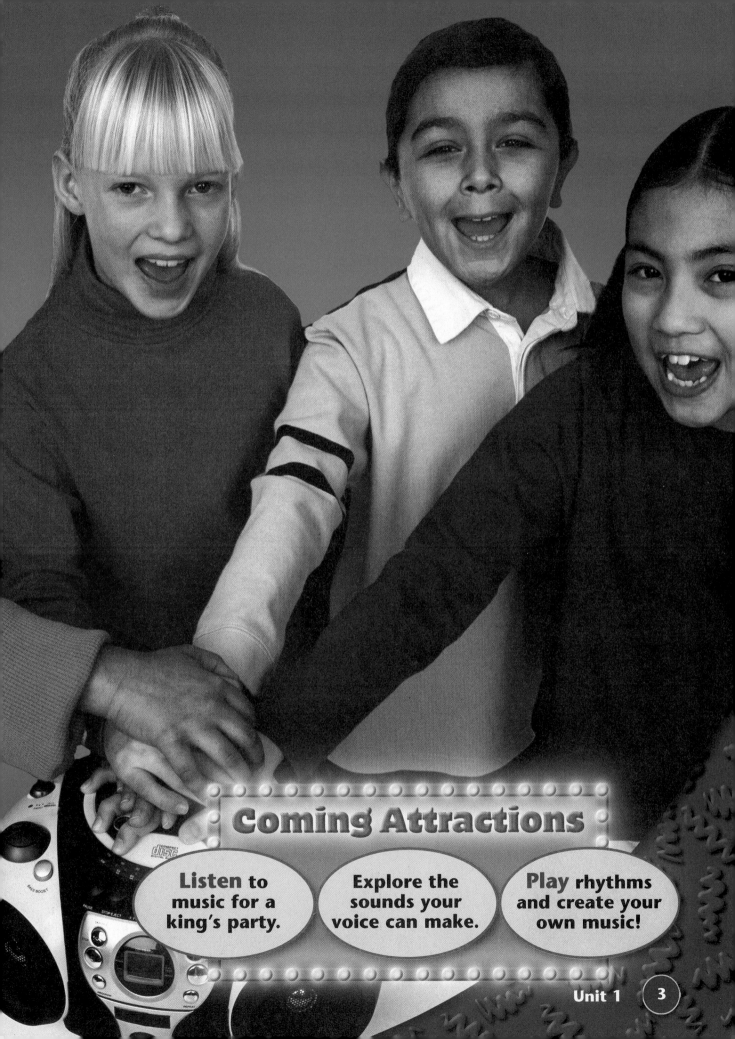

Coming Attractions

Listen to music for a king's party.

Explore the sounds your voice can make.

Play rhythms and create your own music!

There are many games you can play with music. Here is a musical way to play Simon Says. **Sing** as you move to the words.

SIMON SAYS

CD 01:01

Words and Music by Elliot Chiprut

Verse

G

1. I'd   like   to   play   a   game___   that   is
2. Sim - ple   Si - mon   says,___   "Put   your
3. Now   that   you   have   learned   to   play   this

Am   D

so   much   fun,___ and   it's   not___   so   ver - y   hard   to   do.___
hands on your hips."_ "Let   your   back - bone   slip,"___   Si - mon   says._
game with   me,___ you   can   see___   it's   not   so   hard   to   do.___

CONCEPT
RHYTHM
SKILLS
SING,
MOVE
LINKS
READING,
LANGUAGE ARTS

Follow the Rhythm

Children all over the world have fun with singing games. Learn this new singing game. Then have more fun when you teach the game to a friend.

Sing the counting song "Billy."

Move to the first words of the song "Billy."
Point out these words in this song.

Look at the pictures and learn how to move to the words. **Move** to the song as you sing it again.

cross	down	when

Billy

CD 1:4

Swing Rhythm   Children's Clapping Game

Cross down when Bil - ly was
- (1.) one,
- (2.) two,
- (3.) three,
- (4.) four,
- (5.) five,

he learned to
- jump and
- tie his
- climb a
- shut the
- swim and

run. — Run ↑ ol - ly ol - ly, run ↑ ol - ly ol - ly,
shoes. — Shoes — shoes
tree. — Tree — tree
door. — Door — door
dive. — Dive — dive

half past
- one,
- two,
- three,
- four,
- five,

cross down when twelve.

6. Cross down when Billy was six, he learned to pick up sticks . . .
7. Cross down when Billy was seven, he learned to look to heaven . . .
8. Cross down when Billy was eight, he learned to rollerskate . . .
9. Cross down when Billy was nine, he learned to sing so fine . . .
10. Cross down when Billy was ten, he learned to start again . . .
11. Cross down when Billy was eleven, he learned to count to seven . . .
12. Cross down when Billy was twelve, he learned to ring the bell . . .

Where's the Beat?

Listen to this poem about an elephant. Then slowly say the poem and tap your foot once when you say the words or parts of words in yellow. Don't stop, speed up, or slow down. Your foot is tapping with the **beat** . The beat is always steady.

Way Down South

CD 1:7

Anonymous

Way down south where ba-na-nas grow,

A grass-hop-per stepped on an el-e-phant's toe.

The el-e-phant said, with tears in his eyes,

"Pick on some-bo-dy your own size."

8

Listen for some words with long sounds and some words with short sounds. The long and short sounds you hear are called the **rhythm** of the words. Say the poem and clap the rhythm of the words.

Way	down	south	where ba-	na-	nas	grow,

A	grass-	hop- per	stepped	on an	el- e-	phant's	toe.

The	el- e-	phant	said,	with	tears	in his	eyes,

"Pick	on	some-	bo- dy	your	own	size."

THINK! How do beat and rhythm of the words differ?

The Shape of Melody

CONCEPT
MELODY
SKILLS
LISTEN,
SING
LINKS
HISTORY,
CULTURE

"Chan mali chan" is a popular song from Singapore. It tells the story of a baby goat walking to town. He talks with people he meets along the way. The words do not mean anything at all—they are just fun to sing! **Sing** the song.

MAP

UNITED STATES

SINGAPORE →

CD 1:10

Singaporean Folk Song

Sing "Chan mali chan" again. On what words does the tune go upward? On what words does the tune go downward? On what words does the tune repeat the same notes?

chan mali chan

oi oi

Verse 4

G   C   G

1. Di - ma - na di - a   a - nak kam - bing sa - ya
    di ma na di   a   a   nak kam bing sa   ya
2. Di - ma - na di - a   a - nak kam - bing sa - ya
    di ma na di   a   a   nak kam bing sa   ya

D   G

A - nak kam - bing sa - ya   per - gi   ke Ko - ta Bha - ru;
a   nak kam bing sa   ya   pe gi   ke ko ta ba   ɾu
A - nak kam - bing sa - ya   ma - kan   te - pi pe - ri - gi;
a   nak kam bing sa   ya   ma kan   ta pi pe ɾi   gi

G   C   G

Di - ma - na di - a   chin - ta   ha - ti   sa - ya
di ma na di   a   chin ta   ha ti   sa   ya
Di - ma - na di - a   chin - ta   ha - ti   sa - ya
di ma na di   a   chin ta   ha ti   sa   ya

D   G   *D.C. al Fine*

chin ta ha - ti   sa - ya   yang pa - kai ba - ju bi - ru.
chin ta ha ti   sa   ya   yang pa   kai ba ju   bi   ru
chin ta ha - ti   sa - ya   yang ti - dak a - da gi - gi.
chin ta ha ti   sa   ya   yang ti· dak a da gi   gi

Trace the Tune

"A String of Pearls" is a dance tune that was popular in the 1930s. Many people still enjoy the melody and listen to this music today. A **melody** is a string of connected pitches moving upward, downward, or repeating the same pitches. **Pitch** is the highness or lowness of a sound. Every melody has a shape.

Listen to "A String of Pearls." Trace the shape of the melody by pointing to each pearl on the string.

 LISTENING CD 1:14

A String of Pearls by Glenn Miller

Listening Map for A String of Pearls

Glenn Miller used an orchestra to play his music. Besides writing his own music and conducting it, Miller also played the trombone. Listen for the trombone in "A String of Pearls."

MIDI

For another activity with "I's the B'y," see *Spotlight on MIDI*.

"I's the B'y" is a fun song from the island of Newfoundland. It is about a fisherman's busy job catching fish. Look at the melody. Some of the pitches go upward, some go downward, and some repeat. **Sing** this song. Listen to the words *I's the b'y that*. Does the melody go upward, downward, or stay the same?

MAP

UNITED STATES — NEWFOUNDLAND

I's the B'y

CD 1:15

Newfoundland Folk Song

Verse

1. I's the b'y that builds the boat, And I's the b'y that sails her!
2. Sods and rinds to cov-er your flake,__ Cakes and tea for sup-per,
3. I don't want your mag-got-y fish,__ That's no good for win-ter,

I's the b'y that catch-es the fish, And brings them home to Liz - er.
Cod-fish in the spring o' the year,__ Fried in mag-got-y but - ter.
I could buy as good__ as that__ Down in Bon - a - vis - ta.

Refrain

Hip your part-ner, Sal - ly Tib - bo, Hip your part-ner, Sal - ly Brown!

Fo-go, Twil-lin-gate, Mor-ton's Har-bour, All a - round the cir - cle.

Rhythm Around the House

CONCEPT
RHYTHM
SKILLS
SING, READ, LISTEN
LINKS
READING, VISUAL ARTS

Did you know that you can use things around your house to make music? Years ago people used things they found around the house as instruments. They found that even spoons could make music! Name some things in your classroom that you could use.

Listen to "Great Big House," a song from Louisiana. Listen for the sound of the spoons. **Sing** the song.

CD 1:18

Louisiana Play-Party Song

Great big house in New Or - leans, For - ty sto - ries high; ___
Went down to the old mill stream, To fetch a pail of wa - ter;
Fare thee well, my dar - ling girl, Fare thee well, my daugh - ter;

Ev' - ry room that I been in, Filled with chick - en pie.
Put one arm a - round my wife, The o - ther 'round my daugh - ter.
Fare thee well, my dar - ling girl, with the gol - den slip - pers on her.

The "drummer" in this group of musicians is playing pie tins and a washboard, as well as a kazoo.

The rhythm of "Great Big House" uses one sound, two sounds, and even no sounds to the beat.

one sound	two sounds	no sounds
♩	♫	𝄾
quarter note	**eighth notes**	**quarter rest**
the word *pie*	the word *chicken*	no words

Clap this rhythm as you say *pie* for each quarter note (♩) and *chicken* for each pair of eighth notes (♫).

Play the rhythm on a rhythm instrument while saying *chicken* and *pie*. Repeat the rhythm on rhythm instruments while you sing "Great Big House."

Look at the music below. Find the **bar lines**. How many are there? The space between the bar lines is called a **measure**. Next, find the **meter signature**. The top number shows how many beats are in each measure. How many beats are in these measures?

Rhythm All Around

This Creole folk song is also from Louisiana. **Listen** to "Sweet Potatoes." You will hear a washboard used as percussion.

=Sweet Potatoes=

CD 1:21

Louisiana Creole Folk Song

1. Soon   as   we   all   cook   sweet po - ta - toes,
2. Soon   as   sup - per's   gone,   Mam - ma   calls   us,
3. Soon's   we   touch   our   heads   to   the   pil - low,
4. Soon's   the   roost - er   crow   in   the   morn - ing,

sweet po - ta - toes,   sweet po - ta - toes.
Mam - ma   calls   us,   Mam - ma   calls   us.
to   the   pil - low,   to   the   pil - low.
in   the   morn - ing,   in   the   morn - ing.

Soon   as   we   all   cook   sweet po - ta - toes,
Soon   as   sup - per's   gone,   Mam - ma   calls   us,
Soon's   we   touch   our   heads   to   the   pil - low,
Soon's   the   roost - er   crow   in   the   morn - ing,

Eat   'em   while   they're   hot.
Get   a - long   to   bed.
Go   to   sleep   right   smart!
Got - ta   wash   our   face.

The rhythm of "Sweet Potatoes" uses quarter notes, eighth notes, and quarter rests. Look at the song. How many quarter rests are there?

For another activity with "Sweet Potatoes," see *Spotlight on MIDI*.

 THINK! **How many beats are in each measure of "Sweet Potatoes"?**

You can play these pitches on instruments. The pitches go with "Sweet Potatoes."

Play the pitches as you sing the song.

CONCEPT
MELODY
SKILLS
LISTEN, SING, PLAY
LINKS
READING

Imagine that you are walking along. A song that you like pops into your head. You start to sing quietly to yourself. Then you begin to sing more loudly. Your steps start to match the beat of the song. How do you feel?

Listen to "The Happy Wanderer." How does the singer feel about hiking in the mountains?

The Happy Wanderer

CD 1:24

Music by Friedrich W. Möller
Words by Antonia Ridge

Verse

1. I love to go a - wan - der - ing,
2. I love to wan - der by the stream
3. I wave my hat to all I meet,
4. High o - ver - head, the sky - lark wing,

A - long the moun - tain track, And as I go,
That danc - es in the sun, So joy - ous - ly
And they wave back to me, And black - birds call
They nev - er rest at home, But just like me,

I love to sing, My knap - sack on my back.____
it calls to me, "Come! Join my hap - py song."____
so loud and sweet From ev - ery green - wood tree.____
they love to sing, As o'er the world we roam.____

The last three words of "The Happy Wanderer" use three pitches. Trace the melodic shape of *on my back*.

The three pitches you sing for *on my back* are called *mi*, *re*, and *do*. **Sing** "The Happy Wanderer." Sing the pitch syllables *mi, re,* and *do* instead of the words *on my back*.

Sing the song again, and use the hand signs shown in the pictures for *mi, re,* and *do*.

mi

re

do

Show Me the Notes

Pitches are written on a **staff** that has five lines and four spaces. The lines and spaces of the staff are numbered from bottom to top.

In which space is the first note?
Which line goes through the second note?

This staff shows the pitches *mi, re,* and *do* that you sang on the words *chicken pie* in "Great Big House" on p. 14.

mi   re   do

In which space is *mi?* On which line is *re?* In which space is *do?*

Listen to "The Happy Wanderer" again. **Sing** the pitch syllables of the playalong as you listen. **Play** the notes on a pitched instrument.

Playalong

Play with refrain

re   re   re   re   do   do   do   mi   re   re   re   re   mi   re   do   mi

re   re   re   re   do   do   do   mi   re   re   mi   re   do

Different Sounds, Same Voice

CONCEPT
VOCAL TONE COLOR

SKILLS
SING, COMPARE, PERFORM

LINKS
READING, CULTURE

Your voice can make different sounds. You can use your voice to speak, whisper, shout, and sing.

This song is a counting song, like "Billy" on page 6. It is about counting apples, and it comes from Hungary. **Listen** to this song. Are the performers using their speaking, whispering, or singing voices?

Perform this song with your singing voice.

MAP

UNITED STATES   HUNGARY

Egy üveg alma

One Jar of Apples

 CD 1:27

Hungarian Folk Song
English Words by Mary Goetze

Hungarian: Egy ü - veg al - ma, Két ü - veg al - ma,
Pronunciation: ɛdy ü vɛg al ma ket ü vɛg al ma
English: One jar of ap - ples, Two jars of ap - ples,

Há-rom ü - veg al - ma, Négy ü - veg al - ma,
ha ɾom ü vɛg al ma nɛdy ü vɛg al ma
Three jars of ap - ples, Four jars of ap - ples,

Öt ü - veg al - ma Hat ü - veg al - ma,
öt ü vɛg al ma hat ü vɛg al ma
Five jars of ap - ples, Six jars of ap - ples,

This chart shows the numbers one to ten in English and in Hungarian.

Pair up with a friend.

One speaks the numbers in Hungarian and the other whispers the same numbers in English.

Listen to the song again to hear all the numbers sung in Hungarian.

	1	2	3	4	5
English	one	two	three	four	five
Hungarian	egy	két	három	négy	öt

	6	7	8	9	10
English	six	seven	eight	nine	ten
Hungarian	hat	hét	nyolc	kilenc	tíz

Hét ü - veg al - ma, Nyolc ü - veg al - ma,
het ü vɛg al ma nyolts ü vɛg al ma
Sev-en jars of ap - ples, Eight jars of ap - ples,

Ki - lenc ü - veg al - ma, Tíz ü - veg al - ma,
ki lɛnts ü vɛg al ma tiz ü vɛg al ma
Nine_ jars of ap - ples, Ten jars of ap - ples,

Tíz, tíz, tisz - ta víz, Ha nem tisz - ta, vidd visz - sza
tiz tiz tis ta viz ha nɛm tis ta vid vis sa
Ten, ten, wa - ter's clean, Dir - ty wa - ter, take it back,

Ott a sza - már meg - isz - sza.
ot a sa maɾ mɛg is sa
Let the don - key drink it up.

Choose a Voice

Silently read this poem from Hungary.

Apple Tree

Apple tree, apple tree,
Will your apple fall on me?
I won't cry and I won't shout
If your apple knocks me out.

—*Anonymous*

Perform "Apple Tree" using the rhythm shown below. How does this change the way you speak the poem?

Ap - ple tree, ap - ple tree, will your ap - ple fall on me?

I won't cry and I won't shout if your ap - ple knocks me out.

Think about the words for which you might use your speaking, whispering, or singing voice. You could whisper *apple tree* the second time you say it. Then it would sound like an echo. Practice how you would like to perform this poem for the class with a partner.

Gathering Apples

Lajos Karcsay (1860–1932) was born in Hungary. Growing up, he wanted very much to be a painter. When Karcsay was 18 years old he moved to Germany to study at an art school. He lived in Germany, but he showed his paintings in Hungary.

The Color of Music

CONCEPT
TONE COLOR
SKILLS
LISTEN, ANALYZE, DESCRIBE
LINKS
READING, HISTORY

Many things have their own special sound. Think about your school. You know the sound of footsteps in the hall, the crunching of paper, and the ring of the school bell. Instruments and voices have their own special sounds too. This sound is called **tone color**.

Follow the map as you listen to "Hornpipe" from *Water Music Suite* by George Frideric Handel.

Meet the Musician

George Frideric Handel (1685–1759) lived most of his life in England. He was a composer and conductor who wrote a large number of songs for voice and other instruments. In 1717, Handel wrote this music for a party that King George I of England was hosting on several boats on the River Thames. The king liked the music so much that the musicians played it over and over as the party boats floated up and down the river. For this reason, this set of pieces is called *Water Music*.

 LISTENING CD 1:31

Hornpipe (excerpt) from *Water Music Suite*

by George Frideric Handel

Each barge on the next page has a different group of instruments on it. You can tell when the music gets to each new barge by the instrumental tone color. When all of the instruments play together, you'll see the Italian word *tutti* on the barge.

Listen to the instruments as you look at the listening map. Why do you think Handel put certain instruments together?

Log on to **music.mmhschool.com** to learn more about Handel.

Listening Map for Hornpipe
from *Water Music Suite*

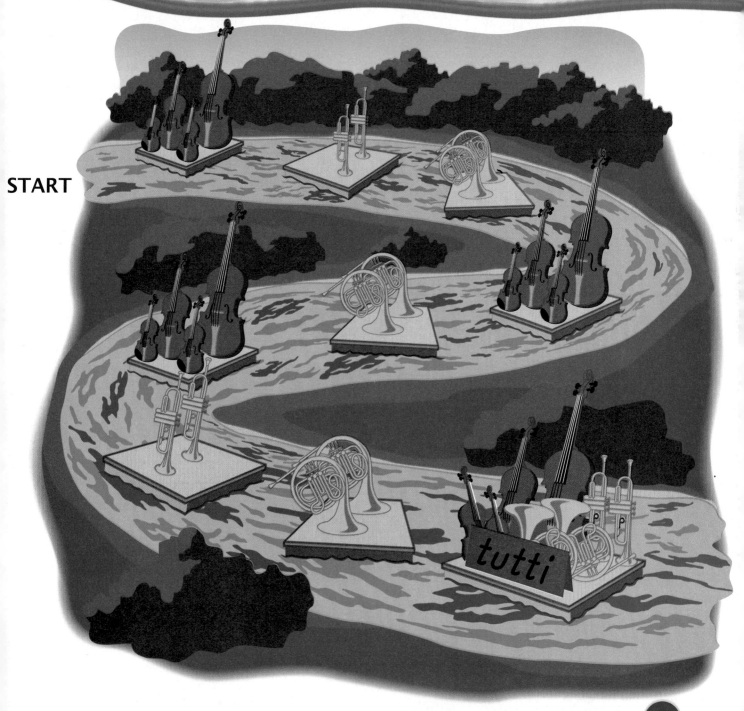

START

tutti

Tone Color

"When I First Came to This Land" tells a story that includes many characters.

Tone color is a good way to tell the characters in this story apart.

Sing the song and learn the story.

When I First Came to This Land

CD 1:32

Words and Music by
Oscar Brand

Verse

1.-5. When I first came to this land, I was not a wealth-y man.

Then I built my-self a shack.
Then I bought my-self a cow.
Then I bought my-self a horse. } I did what I could.
Then I got my-self a wife.
Then I got my-self a son.

Repeat these four measures for additional lines in verses 2-5

I { called my shack   Break-my-back. }
   called my cow   No-milk-now,
   called my horse   Lame-of-course,   } I
   called my wife   Joy-of-my-life.
   told my son   My work's done.

Refrain

Still the land was sweet and good, I did what I could.

28

This playalong gives each character tone color. Every character will have its own instrumental sound.

Playalong

THINK! What instruments would you use for the characters in the song "When I First Came to This Land"? Why?

Rhythm of the Andes

CONCEPT
RHYTHM
SKILLS
LISTEN, MOVE,
IDENTIFY
LINKS
SOCIAL STUDIES,
CULTURE

Learn About Carnaval

Carnaval in the Andes Mountains is a time for celebration. People wear fancy, colorful clothes. They play lots of music. Name some times or events when you celebrate with music.

Listen to "Guadalquivir," which is often heard at Carnaval time.

 LISTENING CD 2:1

Guadalquivir Andean Dance Song

People from different cultures live in the Andes today. They share their culture through the music they play. Some of the rhythms and melodies in the music have been created by people from Spain.

Quechua men playing flute at village festival

Quechua woman playing siku (panpipes)

siku

quena

charango

In "Guadalquivir," you heard different sounds made by different kinds of instruments. These instruments can be put in three different groups: string, wind, and percussion.

String Instruments
String instruments have strings that are plucked, strummed, or bowed.

| violin | banjo | guitar |

Wind Instruments
A wind instrument makes sound when someone blows through it.

| clarinet | recorder | siku |

Percussion Instruments
Percussion instruments make sound when you hit them or shake them.

| snare drum | tambourine | bombo |

Clapping Rhythms

Listen to this song from Peru. Do you hear the *bombo*, a drum from Peru? Now sing "De aquel cerro."

MAP

UNITED STATES

PERU

De aquel cerro

On the Darkened Hillside

CD 2:3

Peruvian Folk Song
Collected by R. and M. D'Harcourt

		F						Dm			Dm7	

Spanish: **En el cer - ro ne - gro ca - en las ne - bli - nas**
Pronounciation: en el se ɾo ne gɾo ka en las ne βli nas
English: **On the dark-ened hill - side, fog is gent - ly fall - ing.**

Dm7   F   Dm   B♭maj7   Am7   Dm

De tus lin - dos o - jos, a - guas cris - ta - li - nas.
ðe tus lin dos o xos a gwas kɾis ta li nas
From your eyes so love - ly, crys - tal tears are flow - ing.

Bombo and siku players

Music from the Andes has special rhythms. Here are two rhythms you heard in "Guadalquivir" and "De aquel cerro."

THINK! What makes music from the Andes Mountains different from "Billy," "Great Big House," and "The Happy Wanderer"?

Musicians from Ecuador

Art Gallery

quenas

Carnaval

Haydee Mendizabal has studied art in South America and in the United States. People from all over the world have seen her works of art.

CONCEPT
RHYTHM
SKILLS
SING, ANALYZE, COMPOSE
LINKS
CULTURE, DANCE

All songs have rhythm. One of the rhythms you know is ♫ You heard this rhythm in "Egy üveg alma," "Simon Says," and "The Happy Wanderer." Name some other songs you know that have this rhythm. This is a fun song from South Africa. How many ♫s are in this song?

Hey, Motswala

MAP

UNITED STATES

SOUTH AFRICA

CD 2:8

South African Folk Song

Refrain

Hey, Mots-wa - la.   Hey, Mots-wa - la.

Hey, Mots-wa - la.   Hey, Mots-wa - la.

End (Fine)

Verse

1. My moth-er trav-elled to Pre-to-ri-a to
2. Her fa-ther wants to give the bride a-way. I
3. And now the time has come, I have to go. I

Go back to the beginning and sing to the End (Da Capo al Fine)

buy the li-cense for the wed-ding day.
think he's wait-ing for a dow - ry.
wish per-haps I had-n't hur-ried so.

You can sing "Hey, Motswala." Look at the pictures and learn how to move to "Hey, Motswala"!

Sing the song. **Move** to the words.

| My | mother | travelled | to |

 LISTENING CD 2:11

Pata Pata by Miriam Makeba and Jerry Ragovoy

 Meet the Musician

Miriam Makeba (b. 1932) was born in South Africa. She is a well-known singer all over the world. In the United States she has performed for the President, starred on Broadway, and recorded many albums. She lived in the United States for many years. She returned to South Africa in 1980.

Create Some Rhythm

You have learned a lot about rhythm. You have learned that a beat can have one sound, two sounds, and no sounds. **Clap** these rhythms.

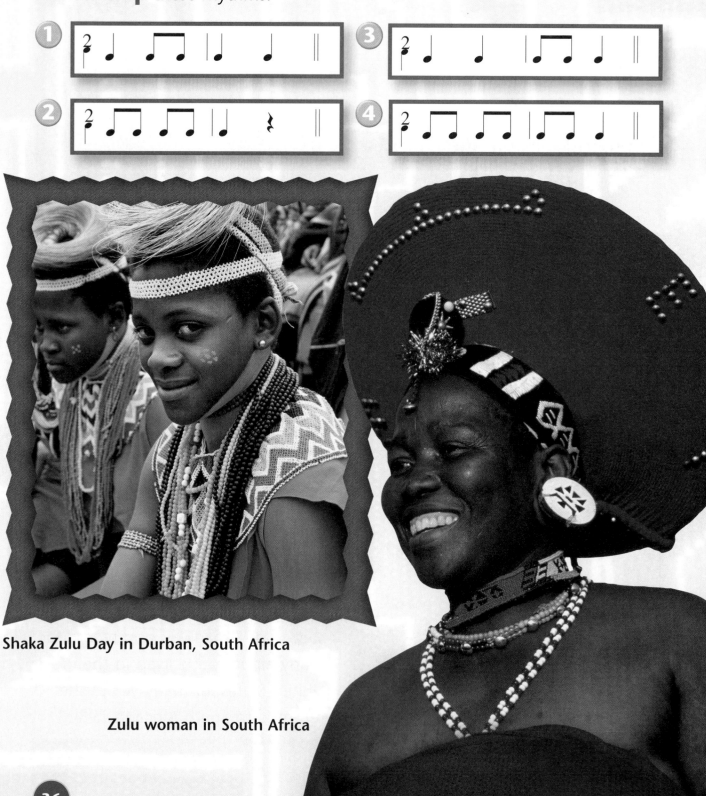

Shaka Zulu Day in Durban, South Africa

Zulu woman in South Africa

Use what you know about rhythms to make your own music. **Create** a rhythm piece that has eight beats in all.

East African cowhide drum

1 Use ♩, ♫, and 𝄽

2 Choose your own order for the beats of your rhythm.

3 Write your rhythm on paper.

4 Use the meter signature ² for your rhythm pattern.

5 Be sure each measure has two beats.

Share your music with the class.

Clap your rhythm piece.

Speak your rhythm piece. Use the word *pie* for the quarter notes and *chicken* for the eighth notes.

Play your rhythm piece on a rhythm instrument.

Spotlight Your Success!

REVIEW

1 What do you call a group of pitches that moves higher, lower, or stays the same?

    a. pitch   **b.** melody   **c.** rhythm   **d.** beat

2 If the meter signature of a song is $\frac{2}{4}$, how many beats are in the measure?

    a. 3   **b.** 8   **c.** 4   **d.** 2

3 This staff shows the pitches *mi*, *re*, and *do*. How does this melody move?

    a. higher   **b.** lower   **c.** stays the same

READ AND LISTEN

CD 2:1

1 **Read** these rhythms. Then **listen**. Which do you hear?

2 **Listen** to this melody. With your index finger, trace the shape of the melody in the air. How did the melody move?

    a. upward   **b.** downward   **c.** stayed the same

3 **Read** these melodies with *do*, *re*, and *mi*. **Listen** to the melody. Which melody do you hear?

a.

b.

c.

THINK!

1 How do beat and rhythm of the words differ?

2 The shape of a melody moves upward. How would the pitches of the melody appear on a musical staff?

3 **Write** about the tone color of an instrument you like.

CREATE AND PERFORM

Create your own melody.

1 Use ⅔ for your meter signature.

2 Use ♩, ♫, and 𝄽 to create your rhythm pattern.

3 Use *mi*, *re*, and *do* for your pitches.

4 **Write** your melody on a piece of paper.

5 Quietly practice what you wrote.

Perform your own melody.

FROM THE TOP

Meet the Musician

ON NATIONAL RADIO!

Names: Ariana and Rexton Park
Ages: 10 and 11
Instrument: Piano
Hometown: Lexington, Massachusetts

Before Ariana and Rexton Park started playing piano, they used to bicker all the time. "We would quarrel for no reason at all," says eleven-year-old Rexton. "The more we play piano, the less we seem to fight." Ten-year-old Ariana agrees. "The piano has changed us!" she says.

Ariana and Rexton are now so close, they sometimes find themselves saying the same thing at the same time. "Our imaginations are alike," explains Rexton. The two enjoy spending time together, especially when they are playing piano duets.

 LISTENING CD 2:13–15 **RECORDED INTERVIEW**

The Funny Road by David Dvorin

Listen to Ariana and Rexton's performance and interview on the national program **From the Top**.

When Jimmy Kane started his part-time job in college, he never realized it would become his full-time career.

Mr. Kane only played guitar and piano before he began working in a family-owned music store. At first, he sold music and instruments. But customers also brought broken instruments for repair, and Mr. Kane's duties changed.

By watching others do repairs, Mr. Kane learned much more about instruments. Today he fixes many types of instruments. He can even play a little on all of them.

Mr. Kane is sure you can learn by experience. He says, "You need a teacher who knows the instrument and to practice *every* day."

Did You Know?

Guitar players produce sound by plucking the six strings.

The guitar's soundboard, the flat surface next to the strings, makes the vibrations of the strings sound louder and clearer.

The guitar is widely used in popular music, but many classical pieces were written for it.

 LISTENING CD 2:16–17

Jesu, Joy of Man's Desiring
by Johann Sebastian Bach

Concierto de Aranjuez, First Movement (excerpt)
by Joaquin Rodrigo

Listen to two pieces. Although not originally for guitar, Bach's music has been adapted for it. Rodrigo's concerto uses melodies that give it a Gypsy sound.

UNIT 2

The World Around You

The sounds of music are all around you. You hear music in nature. You hear music in the sounds of the city. You can hear music in the sounds of voices. All you have to do is listen!

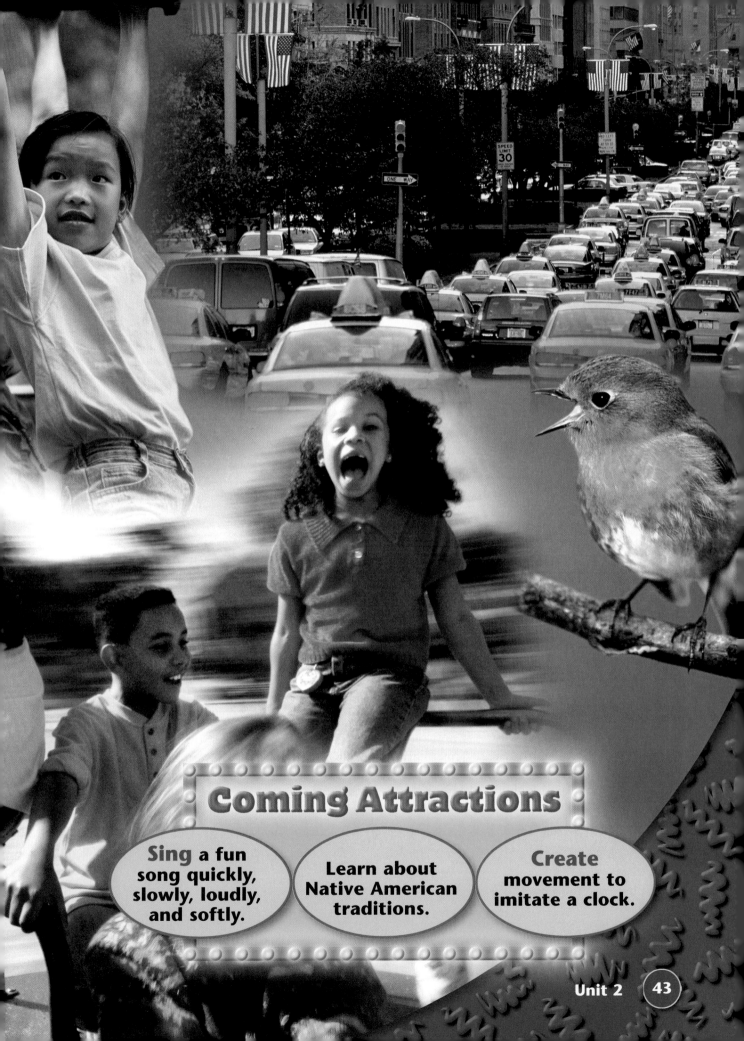

Coming Attractions

Sing a fun song quickly, slowly, loudly, and softly.

Learn about Native American traditions.

Create movement to imitate a clock.

As you listen to this song, make a list of the everyday sounds that it mentions. **Sing** "Music of the World A-Turnin'."

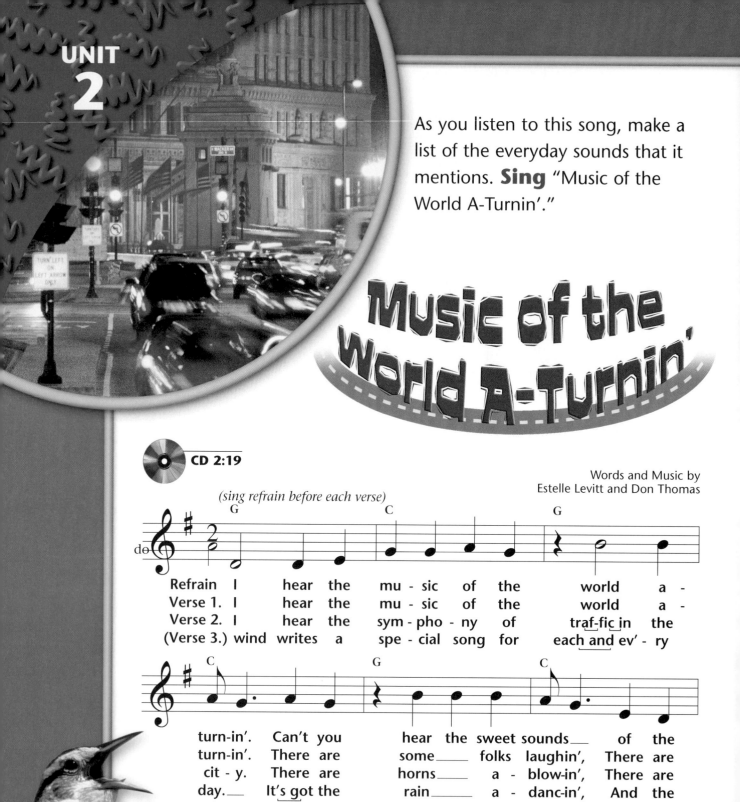

Music of the World A-Turnin'

CD 2:19

Words and Music by
Estelle Levitt and Don Thomas

(sing refrain before each verse)

Refrain   I   hear the   mu - sic   of   the   world   a -
Verse 1.   I   hear the   mu - sic   of   the   world   a -
Verse 2.   I   hear the   sym - pho - ny   of   traf-fic in   the
(Verse 3.) wind   writes   a   spe - cial   song   for   each and ev' - ry

turn-in'.   Can't you   hear   the sweet sounds___   of   the
turn-in'.   There are   some___   folks   laughin',   There are
cit - y.   There are   horns___   a - blow-in',   There are
day.___   It's got the   rain___   a - danc-in',   And the

world   a - turn-in'?_____   Stop,   look and
some   folks   cry - in', _____   Kids   play - in'
heels   a - click-in', _____   Ash   cans   a -
thun-der   a - clap-pin', _____   Don't   just   ig -

lis - ten;   you   can   hear____things a - grow - in'._____
in the   street   sound   sweet - er than   a   cho - ir._____
rat - tlin'   as   the   sun be - gins to   ri - se,_____
nore it: there's   a   con - cert all   a - round you._____

You____ can have mu - sic   wher - ev - er you   go.
(1.-3.) All   you got - ta   do____   is   lis - ten to hear.   3. The

Before you put a toy together, write a story, or have a party, you need a plan. Before a song or piece of music is created, there is a plan. In music, this plan is called **form**. The form for "El florón" has one section. This section is given the letter A.

El florón

The Flower

CD 2:22

Mexican Game Song
English Version by MMH

Spanish: El flo - rón es - tá en las ma - nos, Y en las
Pronounciation: el flo ron es ta en las ma nos yen las
English: In my hand is a love - ly flow - er, Pret - ty

ma - nos es - tá el flo - rón. A - di - vi - nen quién lo
ma nos es ta el flo ron a ði ßi neng kyen lo
flow - er I hold in my hand. Now, I won - der who will

tie - ne, O se que - da de plan - tón.
tye ne o se ke ða ðe plan ton
have it, Or will it stay in my hand?

When a song has two sections that are the same, the form is AA. When the two sections of a song are different, the form is AB. **Listen** to "Nigun Atik." How many different sections do you hear?

 LISTENING CD 2:26

Nigun Atik Israeli Folk Dance

The music for this folk dance has two different sections that take turns like this: ABABA. The dance to "Nigun Atik" also has different movements for the A and B sections to match the music.

The Form Is Set

All music has form. **Listen** to "Sun Don't Set in the Mornin'." How many sections do you hear? Are any of them the same? Which of these describes the form?

AAA   ABA   ABB

CD 2:27

Virginia Folk Song

A

Sun don't set in the morn-in', Sun don't set in the morn-in', Lord,

Sun don't set in the morn-in', Light shines round the world.

B

Sing on,____ sing-in' sis-ter, Sing on,____ sing-in' sis-ter

48

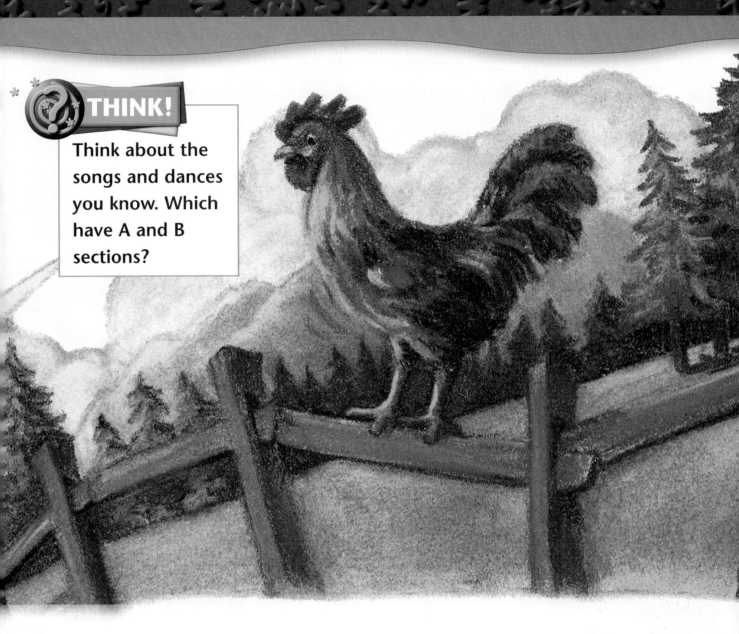

THINK!

Think about the songs and dances you know. Which have A and B sections?

Sing on,___ sing-in' sis-ter, Light shines round the world.

A

Sun don't set in the morn-in', Sun don't set in the morn-in', Lord,

Sun don't set in the morn-in', Light shines round the world.

CONCEPT
RHYTHM
SKILLS
LISTEN, READ, SING
LINKS
READING, DANCE

There are many ways to honor people for how they help others. They can receive a medal or a statue. Some people are honored by having buildings named after them. What are some other ways people are honored? You will hear a story that the Iroquois people tell to honor a special animal.

Listen to this ancient Iroquois story honoring the rabbit.

 LISTENING CD 3:1

Tehahontanekenhnêha' (Rabbit Dance Story)
Iroquois Story
In this story, the rabbit is remembered for the many ways it helps the Iroquois people.

cornhusk doll

Iroquois dancer

Listen to this song that tells the story "Tehahontanekenhnêha'."

 LISTENING CD 3:2

Tehahontanekenhnêha' (Rabbit Dance Song)

Iroquois Song

Singers from the Iroquois Nation perform this song. It is another way the Iroquois people remember the rabbit for the many ways it helps them.

How many instruments do you hear in this song? Listen to the tone color of the instruments. Name the instruments.

THINK! **How do the instruments help the singers tell the story?**

tree bark rattle

Listen to the song again and **read** the music below. The top line is the music for the rattle. The middle line is the music for the drum. Both the rattle and the drum play eighth notes. **Tap** your foot to the quarter notes in the bottom line.

water drum

Playalong

Rattle

Drum

Foot

beadwork

I Have Reason to Dance

The Iroquois people often dance. They dance for many reasons. They dance to celebrate, to tell a story, or to remember events. The Rabbit Dance is a traditional Iroquois dance.

RECORDED INTERVIEW CD 3:3

Jerry Thundercloud McDonald

Listen to Jerrry Thundercloud McDonald talk about traditional music and dance.

Iroquois dancer

Meet the Musician

Jerry Thundercloud McDonald (b. 1962) is a singer, storyteller, dancer, and actor. He created a group called Peacemakers Drum. Peacemakers Drum is a group of Mohawk Native Americans who perform traditional dances like the Rabbit Dance.

turtle carving

Sing this song. It tells a story about another animal. **Listen** for sounds that last two beats.

Learn About Ucha Tirvarch

The Serrano tribe tells a story about a little bear who would not behave. He had to stay out in the cold all night as punishment.

Ucha Tirvarch

Little Bear Song

CD 3:4

Serrano (Maringa') Indian Lullaby
As Sung by Ernest Siva

Verse

Serrano: U - cha u - cha tir - varch, U - cha u - cha tir -
Pronunciation: ʊ cha ʊ cha tɪr varch ʊ cha ʊ cha tɪr

varch, Kai kwun hai - pant Hai - pant nu - ku - man.
varch kaɪ kwʊn haɪ pənt haɪ pənt nu ku man

Refrain

Ay - a kaich, ay - a kaich, Ay - a kaich ay - a kaich,
ay a kaɪch ay a kaɪch ay a kaɪch ay a kaɪch

A - ay - a, ay - a kai - no, a - ay - a, ay - a -
a ay a ay a kaɪ no a ay a ay a

kai - no, A - ay - a, ay - a kai - no.
kaɪ no a ay a ay a kaɪ no

Unit 2 The World Around You

53

Searching for Pitches

CONCEPT
MELODY
SKILLS
SING, ANALYZE, DESCRIBE
LINKS
READING, CULTURES

Children from all over the world play games. "El florón" is a game that Mexican children play with a small flower. **Listen** to the song and then play the game.

1 Hold your hands behind your back and listen to the song with your eyes closed.

2 At the end of the song, close your hands and open your eyes. The person who was "it" will ask one person at a time to guess who has the flower.

3 Whoever guesses right will be "it" when the game begins again.

Sing the first phrase of "El florón" with pitch names. The tinted pitches are called *so* and *la*. **Move** to show each pitch as you sing "El florón."

do   re   mi   so   la

do

re

mi

so

la

Shepherd, Shepherd

CD 3:8

Swing Rhythm

African American Spiritual

Shep - herd, shep - herd, where'd you lose your sheep?
Shep - herd, shep - herd, where'd your leave your lambs?

Shep - herd, shep - herd, where'd you lose your sheep?
Shep - herd, shep - herd, where'd you leave your lambs?

Shep - herd, shep - herd, where'd you lose your sheep? } O, the
Shep - herd, shep - herd, where'd you leave your lambs? }

sheep all gone a - stray._____ The

sheep all gone__ a - stray._____

Play these rhythms on rhythm instruments while you listen to "Shepherd, Shepherd."

CONCEPT
RHYTHM
SKILLS
SING, ANALYZE, DESCRIBE
LINKS
READING, CULTURES

In Nigeria, Africa, some people fish in long boats. The people in the boats have to row for the boats to move. To help everyone row together, the people might sing a song like "Eh Soom Boo Kawaya."

Look at the notes in "Eh Soom Boo Kawaya," a song from Nigeria. Notes show how many beats there are to a sound. A quarter note (♩) shows one beat to a sound. A **half note** shows two beats to a sound. Find the half notes (♩). **Listen** to the song. Point to the half notes (♩) when you hear them. **Sing** the song.

Nigerian Boat Song

MAP
UNITED STATES
NIGERIA

CD 3:11

Nigerian Song

Vocables: Eh   soom boo   ka - wa - ya   ke - dou   ka - dee.

Eh   soom boo   ka - wa - ya   ke - dou   ka - dee.

Ke - dou   ka - dee   ke - dou   ka - dee.

Read these rhythms. **Clap** and say *light* for each quarter note (♩). Clap and say *mornin'* for each pair of eighth notes (♫). Brush one hand down the other arm and say the word *world* for each half note (♩).

Now add pitch. **Sing** these rhythms with pitch names.

do   mi   so so mi so   la   do   mi   do   so   do

ah

Soom boo   ka - wa - ya   ke - dou   ka - dee.

Countermelody

Listen to "Sun Don't Set in the Mornin'." This song has a **countermelody**. A countermelody is a separate melody that fits with the main melody. Both the main melody and the countermelody are performed at the same time. **Sing** this countermelody.

Sun Don't Set in the Mornin'

CD 2:30

Virginia Folk Song
Countermelody by Mary Goetze

Sun don't set in the morn-in', Sun don't set in the morn-in' Lord,

Countermelody

Sun don't set in the morn - in',

Sun don't set in the morn-in', Light shines round the world.

Light shines round the world.

Find the half notes (𝅗𝅥) in the countermelody. How many half notes (𝅗𝅥) are there? Are there any half notes in the melody?

To sing this song, two groups of singers are needed. One group sings the melody. Another group sings the countermelody. Both groups sing at the same time.

Sing "Sun Don't Set in the Mornin'" with the countermelody.

Playalong

Play this part on pitched instruments. Then form three groups. One group can play the instrument part. One group can sing the melody. A third group can sing the countermelody. Now there are three groups performing at the same time!

LESSON 5

The Nature of Sound

CONCEPT
DYNAMICS
SKILLS
SING, LISTEN
LINKS
READING,
CULTURES

Some people celebrate things that happen in nature each year. The Japanese people have the Tanabata (Seven Evenings) Festival. This festival grew out of a story about two stars in the sky that come together each year on the night of July 7. Japanese children hope for clear weather that night. If it rains, the stars cannot meet until the next year! **Listen** to the Japanese song "Tanabata."

Sing the song twice. The first time sing loudly. The second time sing softly.

Seven Evenings

CD 3:15

Music by K. Shimousa
Words by H. Gonda and R. Hayashi

Japanese: さ　　さ　　の　　は　　さ　　ら　　さ　　ら
Pronounciation: sa　　sa　　no　　ha　　sa　　ɾa　　sa　　ɾa
English: **Bam - boo　leaves　are　swayed　by　the breeze.**

の　　き　　ば　　に　　ゆ　　れ　　ろ
no　　ki　　ba　　ni　　yu　　ɾe　　ɾu
Stars　peep　out　a　thou - sand　fold,

THINK! **Think about the lyrics as you sing the song loudly and softly. Which way sounds better? Why?**

In music, the word for loud is **forte**. The word for soft is **piano**. When you sang "Tanabata," you sang it first *forte*, then *piano*. You changed the volume. The word for volume in music is **dynamics**. Dynamics make the music more interesting and exciting!

お ほ し さ ま き ら き ら
o ho shi sa ma ki ɾa ki ɾa
Stars shin-ing bright-ly o - ver the trees,

き ん ぎ ん す な ご
ki ṇ gi ṇ su na go
Stars of sil - ver, stars of gold.

Dynamic Sounds

Dynamics make the overture from the opera *William Tell* very exciting. Its composer, Gioacchino Rossini, composed this music to describe a thunder and lightning storm. **Listen** to hear the sounds of the storm. Do you think thunder sounds should be *piano* or *forte*?

Follow the map as you listen to the *William Tell* Overture.

CD-ROM

Use *Orchestral Instruments* **CD-ROM** to learn more about the instruments of the orchestra.

🔘 **LISTENING** CD 3:19

Overture (excerpt) from *William Tell*

by Gioacchino Rossini

Meet the Musician

Gioacchino Rossini (1792–1868) was born in Italy. He wrote his first opera when he was a teenager. His opera *William Tell* was a big success when people heard it for the first time. Today the overture is still very popular.

Listening Map for *William Tell* (Overture) (excerpt)

It's About Time!

CONCEPT
TEMPO

SKILLS
LISTEN, SING, ARRANGE

LINKS
READING, CULTURES

Does the clock in your classroom keep good time? Is it ever slow? Is it ever fast? The parts of a clock need to move at a steady speed so that it can keep good time. The parts should not move too quickly or too slowly. In music, the word for speed is **tempo**. Just like a clock, most music is performed at a steady tempo.

Listen for the tempo in each section of this music.

LISTENING CD 3:20

A Clock at Night by Svyatoslav Miloslavskiy

"A Clock at Night" is played on the piano. The music describes the movements of the parts of a clock.

Create a repeating movement like a clock. Choose one of these ways to move and keep repeating it.

- up and down
- side to side
- back and forth
- round and round

Perform your movement pattern while you listen to "A Clock at Night." Be sure to show the tempo of each section as you move.

Here is more music about a clock. **Sing** this song from France. Make sure you keep a steady tempo.

MAP

UNITED STATES · FRANCE

La cloche

The Clock

CD 3:21

French Round

French: **Din,** **don,** **din,** **don,** **C'est la clo-che du ma-tin,**
Pronounciation: dɛ̃ dõ dɛ̃ dõ sɛ la klɔ ʃə dü ma tɛ̃

Qui sonne au le - ver du jour: Bon - jour, bon - jour!
ki sɔ no lə ve dü ʒur bõ ʒur bõ ʒur

Largo is the word for a slow tempo. **Allegro** is the word for a fast tempo. At what tempo would you sing "La cloche"?

Turn on the Tempo

"John Jacob Jingleheimer Schmidt" is a song all about tempo and dynamics. The tempo of each verse is steady, but each time the song repeats, the song gets faster. How quickly can you sing this song and keep the tempo steady?

John Jacob Jingleheimer Schmidt

CD 3:25

American Camp Song

John Jacob Jing - le - heim - er Schmidt,

His name is my name too.

When - ev - er I go out, the peo - ple al - ways shout,

"There goes John Ja - cob Jing - le - heim - er

Schmidt," Da da da da da da da da.

Last time only

With your class, decide if you will use your singing voice, shouting voice, or whispering voice on the words *Da da da da da da da da*. Change the voice you use every time you sing the verse again.

With your class, decide where to sing *piano* and where to sing *forte*.

Put it all together. **Sing** the song. Remember to change the tempo every time you repeat the verse.

Remember which voice to use on the words *Da da da da da da da da*.

Don't forget where to sing *piano* and *forte*. Good luck!

THINK!

How would you change the tempo from the first time you sing "John Jacob Jingleheimer Schmidt" if you wanted to sing it through many times? Remember that each time you sing the song, it gets faster.

What's the Connection?

CONCEPT
RHYTHM

SKILLS
LISTEN, ANALYZE, COMPOSE

LINKS
CULTURES, DANCE

Look at these dancers. They are showing one way to connect a circle. Many dances are done in a circle. "Nigun Atik" on p. 47 is an Israeli dance done in a circle. When you do the first five steps in the A section of "Nigun Atik," use this handheld position.

Perform the dance to the A section.

Listen to the music again. Clap this rhythm to the B section.

Notes can be connected with a **tie**. A tie is a curved line that connects two notes of the same pitch. It means that the sound of the first note should be held for the length of both notes.

These two quarter notes (♩♩) are tied together. Another way to show a sound that lasts two beats is ♩♩

Clap this rhythm with the B section. Make a two-beat brushing motion down your arm for the tied quarter notes.

Half notes (𝅗𝅥) are also held for two beats. **Clap** this rhythm with the B section.

Make a two-beat brushing motion down your arm for the tied quarter notes and half notes. Both ♩♩ and 𝅗𝅥 will sound the same when you perform them.

Clap this rhythm. Now play this rhythm using instruments. Tapping a metal instrument like the triangle will produce a long, ringing sound. Tapping a drum produces a much shorter sound. **Play** along with the B section of "Nigun Atik."

Israeli men dancing

THINK!

What other rhythm instrument would be a good choice to make sounds that last two beats?

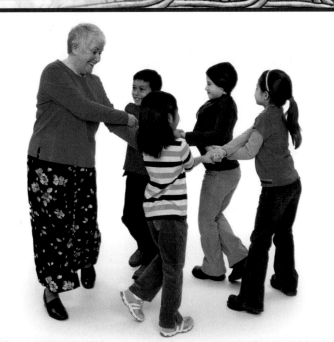

Rattle, Chirp, and Scratch!

Listen for tempo changes in this song from Kentucky.
Sing the song.

CD 3:28

Words and Music by Aunt Molly Jackson

1. Rat-tle-snake,— O, rat-tle-snake,— what makes your teeth so
2. Roost - er,— O, roost - er,— what makes your claws so

faster 3. Jay - bird,— O, jay - bird,— what makes you fly so

white?   I been in the bot - tom
hard?   Been scratch-in' this__ grav - el
high?   Been rob-bin' your__ corn - patch

all my life, an' I ain't done noth - in' but bite,
all my days. It's a won - der I___ ain't tired,
all my life. It's a won - der I___ don't die,

bite,   ain't done noth - in' but bite.
tired,   won - der I___ ain't tired.
die,   won - der I___ don't die.

Identify the words in each verse that are always sung for two beats.

Create an 8-beat rhythm with a partner.

Say *rattle* and clap for eighth notes (♫).

Say *chirp* and clap for quarter notes (♩).

Say *scratch* and brush for half notes (♩).

Arrange your rhythm different ways. Say your rhythm with a steady tempo. **Perform** your 8-beat rhythm for the class.

CONCEPT
FORM
SKILLS
SING, ANALYZE, DESCRIBE
LINKS
READING, ART

Read this poem about sounds you hear in the city.

City Music

Snap your fingers.
Tap your feet.
Step out a rhythm
down the street.

Rap on the litter bin.
Stamp on the ground.
City music
is all around.

Beep says motor-car.
Ding says bike.
City music
is what we like.

—Tony Mitton

A crowing rooster is usually heard on a farm. **Sing** a song about a rooster on the next page. It uses the same idea more than once. This is called **repetition**. One idea combined with a different idea is called **contrast**. Repetition and contrast make music more interesting.

Kum Bachur

CD 3:31   **The Rooster**

Israeli Folk Song

1 C   G7   C

do

Hebrew: קוּם בַּ חוּר עַ צֵל וְ אֵ ל עֲ בוֹ דָה

Pronunciation: kum ba xur a tsel vʼɛ tse la a vo da

English: Now the roost-er's crow-ing, He crows to greet the day.

C   G7   C

קוּם בַּ חוּר עַ צֵל וְ אֵ ל עֲ בוֹ דָה

kum ba xur a tsel vʼɛ tse la a vo da

Now the roost-er's crow-ing, He crows to greet the day.

2 C   G7   C

קוּם קוּם יְ אֵ ל עֲ בוֹ דָה

kum kum vɛ tse la a vo da

Rise, get up, it's time for work and play.

C   G7   C

קוּם קוּם יְ אֵ ל עֲ בוֹ דָה

kum kum vɛ tse la a vo da

Rise, get up, it's time for work and play.

3 C   G7   C

קוּ קוּ רִי קוּ קוּ קוּ רִי קוּ תַר נֶ גוֹל קָ רָא

ku ku ɾi ku ku ku ɾi ku taɾ ɛn gol ka ɾa

Ku - ku - ri - ku, ku - ku - ri - ku, That's what roost-ers say,

C   G7   C

קוּ קוּ רִי קוּ קוּ קוּ רִי קוּ תַר נֶ גוֹל קָ רָא

ku ku ɾi ku ku ku ɾi ku taɾ ɛn gol ka ɾa

Ku - ku - ri - ku, ku - ku - ri - ku, That's what roost-ers say.

Finding Form

Listen for repetition and contrast as you follow the map.

 LISTENING CD 3:35

Ballet of the Unhatched Chicks
from *Pictures at an Exhibition* by Modest Mussorgsky

The form of "Ballet of the Unhatched Chicks" is AABA. The A section repeats, and then the B section makes a contrast. The A section comes back to finish the piece.

Listening Map for Ballet of the Unhatched Chicks

A

First time only

Log on to **music.mmhschool.com** to learn more about Modest Mussorgsky and his music.

B

Spotlight Your Success!

REVIEW

1 Which pattern has half notes in it?

a.

b.

c.

d.

2 The first pitch is *do*. Where is *la*?

a. first space

b. second space

c. third line

3 Why are some sections of music called B?

a. The B section is just like the A section.

b. The B section is different from the A section.

c. The B section is a big section.

READ AND LISTEN

CD 3:36

1 **Listen** to a melody with three sections. Close your eyes. Raise your hand each time you hear the A section. Fold your arms for each B section. What is the form?

a. AAB   b. ABB   c. ABA

2 **Read** these melodies. Then listen. Which melody do you hear?

a.

b.

c.

THINK!

1 What is the difference between *piano* and *forte*?

2 When you are learning to sing a new piece, what tempo would you choose?

3 What would the form be if only contrast were used in a three-section piece of music?

4 **Write** about how dynamics change the feeling of a song.

CREATE AND PERFORM

Create a rhythm with ABA as the form.

1 Use ⁴ for your meter signature.

2 Make each section eight beats long.

3 Use at least one ♩ in each section.

4 Write your rhythm on a piece of paper.
Hint: your rhythm should be six measures long.

Play your rhythm.

Meet the Musician
ON NATIONAL RADIO!

Name: Randall Brown
Age: 18
Instrument: Saxophone
Hometown: Twin Falls, Idaho

The first time Randall Brown saw a musician playing a saxophone, he decided he wanted to play one, too. "How can I get one of those?" he thought.

Randall came up with a plan. He placed a big jar on the counter and labeled it "The Randall Brown Saxophone Fund." Each day, members of his family threw their spare change into the jar. Soon, over $300 had been collected!

"My parents finally saw how serious I was about playing the saxophone," says Randall. On his next birthday, Randall received a shiny new saxophone!

When he's not playing saxophone, Randall enjoys learning magic tricks, playing golf and basketball, in-line skating, and playing computer games with his brothers.

 LISTENING   CD 4:1–2   **RECORDED INTERVIEW**

Sigh of the Soul for Alyscamp from *Tableaux de Provence* (Fourth Movement)
by Paule Maurice

Listen to Randall's performance and interview on the national radio progam From the Top.

A Tip From the Top!
"Make a Plan."
If you're serious about accomplishing something, make a plan. Randall Brown came up with an idea for how he could get a saxophone, and he helped make it happen.

Spotlight on the English Horn

Did You Know?

The English horn, or *cor anglais*, is a double-reed instrument.

The name "English horn" is something of a mystery. Some think that the word *anglias*, for angels, was misspelled as *anglais*, the French word for English, and the name stuck.

An English horn has a curved bocal, the short metal tube that connects the reed to the instrument. On an oboe, the reed is inserted directly into the top of the instrument. An English horn's bell is pear-shaped, but the bell of an oboe flares out.

reed — bocal

keys

bell

 LISTENING CD 4:3–4

Symphony No. 9 ("From the New World"), Largo (excerpt)
by Antonín Dvořák

Polovtsian Dances (excerpt) from *Prince Igor*
by Alexander Borodin

Listen to these beautiful English horn melodies. The first is reminiscent of the African American spirituals Dvořák heard when he visited America. In the dance by Borodin, you will first hear the oboe, the smaller, higher-pitched cousin of the English horn. Then listen for the English horn, which has a deeper, more mellow sound.

Tunes, Tales, and Traditions

People around the world share songs and stories with each other. Sharing helps people become a larger community. Your class is a community. What songs and stories do you share in your class?

Coming Attractions

Sing songs and play games from around the world.

Sing a song from the movie _Pocahontas_.

Learn how to conduct music.

Everyone shares our planet. We are all part of the world community. In the song "Colors of the Wind," Pocahontas teaches respect for everybody and everything. **Sing** "Colors of the Wind."

Colors of the Wind

from the movie *Pocahontas*

CD 4:5

Music by Alan Menken
Lyrics by Stephen Schwartz

1. You   think you own what-ev - er land you   land on;
   think the on - ly peo-ple who are   peo - ple

   the earth is just a dead thing you can   claim;
   are the peo - ple___ who look and think like   you,

   but   I   know ev - 'ry rock and tree and   crea - ture
   but   if you walk the foot-steps of   a   strang - er,

   has   a   life, has a spir - it, has a name.   2. You
   you'll learn

   things you   nev-er knew___ you nev - er   knew.

Have you ev-er heard the wolf cry to the blue corn moon, or

asked the grin-ning bob-cat why he grinned?

Can you sing with all the voic-es of the moun-tain?

Can you paint with all the col-ors of the wind?

Can you paint with all the col-ors of the wind?

mountain

wind

sing

Treasure Your Tradition

CONCEPT
RHYTHM
SKILLS
DESCRIBE,
SING, MOVE
LINKS
DANCE,
CULTURES,
HISTORY

Music is one way that people pass down stories and customs. Sometimes music tells a story with words. Sometimes it tells a story by using the sounds of different instruments.

Look at the pictures of these groups on this page. **Describe** how music is used to tell their stories.

Carnaval, Brazil

Gospel singers, Brooklyn, New York

Tsimshian dancers and drummers, Klallam Reservation, Kingston, Washington

Many groups of people use dance to tell stories. "Raccoon Dance Song" is a Native American song and dance from the Ottawa nation. It honors the raccoon and is usually performed by children.

CD 4:8

Ottawa Native American

Ottawa: Es - si bon__ nin - di - go___ Es - si bon__ nin - di - go___

be - ba - ma - da se - a - ni_____ Sa - sa sa - sa

Go back to the beginning

sa - sa sa - sa i hi hi___ i i___ hi

Gallop and Step!

Sometimes a group uses the same instruments to play most of their music. In Scotland, bagpipes and drums are often used to play music.

Listen for the sounds of the Scottish bagpipes and bodhrán (drum) in "Gi'Me Elbow Room."

Sing this song from Scotland.

Scottish bagpipe players

Gi'Me Elbow Room

CD 4:12

Scottish Folk Song

Cam'-ron he came in-to town and all he want-ed was
el - bow room. (clap)
Oh gi' me el-bow room.___ Oh gi' me el-bow room.
Gi' me el-bow room.___ Oh gi' me el-bow room. Oh

Whisper *gi'me, gi'me* to match the rhythm of your feet as you gallop. First move sideways to the right and then sideways to the left.

Listen to the rhythm of your feet as you step-hop and gallop. Stepping has a different rhythm than galloping.

LOG ON

Log on to **music.mmhschool.com** to learn more about the bagpipes.

When you step-hop on each beat, the rhythm looks like this:

step - hop

When you gallop on each beat, the rhythm looks like this:

gal - lop

THINK!

Which rhythm is equal? Which rhythm is unequal? Why?

CONCEPT
MELODY
SKILLS
SING, MOVE, DESCRIBE
LINKS
FINE ART, CULTURES, DANCE

Many times the things you treasure are not things that you can buy. Maybe your treasures are things that you cannot even see!

Treasure Chests

CD 4:15

Words and Music by Minnie O'Leary

1. Some of us come from a dis-tant land, Some of us from near-
2. Hol - i-days, games and___ stor - ies, Lan-gua-ges and___

by, But all of us car - ry a treas - ure chest With
songs;____ Faith_ and cour - age and wis - dom, And

things that gold can't buy; with things that gold can't buy.
ways to get a - long; and ways to get a - long.

90

This song has two sections: a **verse** and a **refrain**. The words in the verses are different. The words in the refrain stay the same. **Tap** the beat on your knees with both hands during the verse. Tap the beat on your knees one hand at a time during the refrain. Look at the pictures to learn this pattern.

Sing the song and perform the movement.

Look at the arched lines over the melody. These lines are called phrase marks and go over a **phrase**. A phrase is a short section of music that is one musical thought. How many phrases are in this song?

verse

refrain

Refrain C   G

And   when   we   share   our   treas-ure   chests   we

C   D   C   G

all grow rich, you   see.   The rich-es in that treas-ure chest are

Am   D7   C   D7   G

what makes you and   me;   are   what makes you   and   me.

Trace the Phrase

Some phrases are longer than others.
"Les saluts," a French Canadian folk dance,
has a melody with phrases of different lengths.
The A section has two phrases that are each
sixteen beats long. The B section has four
phrases that are each four beats long.

 LISTENING CD 4:18

Les saluts French Canadian Folk dance

Listen to this folk dance.
Trace an arc over your
head for each phrase as
you listen to the music.

 Art Gallery

Fiddler and Boy Doing Jig

Cornelius Krieghoff
(1815–1872) created this oil
painting on canvas in 1852.
It shows a boy dancing to the
music that the man is playing
on the fiddle.

One of the instruments you heard playing the melody of "Les saluts" was the violin. When settlers from Europe and the British Isles came to North America, the violin was often the only instrument they had to play as they sang and danced.

A violin is made of wood. It has four strings and is played by pulling a bow across the strings to make them vibrate. The strings can also be plucked.

Listen to "Les saluts" again.

Describe the sound the violin makes when it plays.

tuning pegs

bow

strings

bridge

chin rest

CD-ROM

Use *Orchestral Instruments* CD-ROM to learn more about the violin.

Step in Time

CONCEPT
RHYTHM
SKILLS
READ, SING, MOVE
LINKS
HISTORY, DANCE

Say the nursery rhyme "Humpty Dumpty" and clap your hands to the rhythm of the words. "Throw It Out the Window" uses the words of different nursery rhymes. **Sing** the song while tapping the beat on your knee.

Throw It Out the Window

CD 4:19

Nursery Rhyme Parody

1. Old Moth - er   Hub - bard___   went   to   the   cup-board   to
2. Old___   King   Cole   was   a   mer - ry   old   soul, and   a
3. Lit - tle   Bo   Peep___   has   lost___   her   sheep,_   and
4. Where,_   oh, where   has   my   lit - tle   dog   gone?__   Oh,
5. Yan - kee   Doo - dle   went__   to   town___   a -

fetch her poor   dog   a   bone.__   But when she got there,   the
mer - ry   old   soul   was he.____   He called for his pipe, and   he
does-n't know where   to   find them. But leave them a - lone;   when
where,_   oh, where can he   be?___ With his ears___   cut short and his
rid - ing   on   a   po - ny;   He stuck___   a   fea - ther

cup - board   was   bare,   so she threw   it
called for   his   bowl,   and__   threw   them
they___   come home she'll_   throw   them
tail___   cut long.   I'll___   throw   him
in___   his   cap   and_   threw   it

out the win - dow, the

Name another nursery rhyme that would fit this song.
Sing this song using the new nursery rhyme.

Read these rhythms. Say *throw it* for ♩♪ and *out* for ♩.

THINK! What movement would fit this song the best: step–hop or gallop? Why?

win-dow, the sec-ond sto-ry win-dow.

But when she got there,   the
He called for his pipe, and he
But leave them a - lone;__when
With his ears__ cut short and his
He stuck__ a fea - ther

cup-board was   bare,   so she threw   it   out   the   win - dow.
called for   his   bowl,   and__ threw them out   the   win - dow.
they__   come home,   she'll__ throw them out   the   win - dow.
tail__   cut   long,   I'll__   throw him   out   the   win - dow.
in__   his   cap   and__ threw   it   out   the   win - dow.

6. A-tisket, a-tasket,
   a green and yellow basket,
   I wrote a letter to my love
   and threw it out the window.
   The window, the second story window,
   I wrote a letter to my love
   and threw it out the window.

Compare These Rhythms

When you dance, you listen to the rhythm of the music to know how to move. "Bransle de Champaigne" is a French dance that was popular almost 500 years ago. **Listen** to this dance. Think about what movements you would do to the music.

 LISTENING CD 4:22

Bransle de Champaigne by Claude Gervaise

"Bransle de Champaigne" has two sections. Listen to the dance again. Look at the rhythms. How many times do you hear the A section? How many times do you hear the B section?

Look at the end of the first A section and the B section. There is a 𝄇 at the end of each section. This sign (𝄇) is called a **repeat sign**. It tells you to perform that section twice. Because of the repeat signs, the form of "Bransle de Champaigne" is AABBA.

Jogging movements are good to use in "Bransle de Champaigne" because there are two equal sounds to each beat (♫ ♫). Galloping is a good movement for "Throw It Out the Window" because the rhythm is made up of unequal sounds. The long-short, long-short rhythm can be written as:

gal - lop   gal - lop   gal - lop   gal - lop

Look at the table to see how the rhythms are different for equal and unequal sounds.

Meter sign	$\frac{2}{4}$	$\frac{2}{4.}$
One sound to a beat	♩	♩.
Two sounds to a beat	♫	♩ ♪

CONCEPT
MELODY

SKILLS
READ, IDENTIFY,
PLAY

LINKS
HISTORY,
LANGUAGE
ARTS, READING

The song "Cumberland Gap" tells the story of pioneers making the long journey through a mountain pass.

Listen to two phrases of the song "Cumberland Gap." How are the phrases different? With your finger, trace the shape of the melody in the air as you listen again.

Sing the blue highlight section using pitch names.
Hum the tan highlight phrase to find the two mystery pitches. Are these pitches higher or lower than the other pitches in the song? The names of the new pitches are **low so** and **low la** . Look at the staff below. Is low *la* in a space or on a line? What about low *so*?

so₁ la₁ do re mi so la

Sing the second phrase of the verse of "Cumberland Gap" using pitch names.

 Art Gallery

Daniel Boone Leading Settlers Through the Cumberland Gap

This painting was created by George Caleb Bingham in 1851. It shows pioneer Daniel Boone guiding settlers to Kentucky through the Cumberland Gap. Pioneers are people that find new places to live. As Americans moved west, the Cumberland Gap became an important passageway for explorers through the Appalachian Mountains.

CD 4:23

Southern Appalachian Folk Song

Verse

1.,3.,5. Me and my   wife   and my   wife's   grand - pap
2. Cum-ber-land   Gap   with it's   cliffs   and   rocks,
4. Cum-ber-land   Gap   is   a   mighty   fine   place.

all   go-in'   down   to   Cum-ber-land   Gap.
home   of the   pan - ther,   bear   and   fox.
Three kinds of   wa - ter to   wash   your   face.

Refrain

Cum-ber-land   Gap,   Cum-ber-land   Gap.

(pat)   (clap)   (snap)   (whoo!)

Way   down___   yon-der   in   Cum-ber-land   Gap.

(hum) _____

Unit 3 Tunes, Tales, and Traditions

99

Mapping out the Music

You have learned about Daniel Boone and the pioneers in the United States. Now you will learn about the *voyageurs* in Canada. *Voyageurs* is a French word for "travellers." These travellers explored Canada in canoes hundreds of years ago. To help them keep a steady beat in their paddling, *voyageurs* sang songs like "En roulant ma boule."

The music has been organized with repeat signs, **first endings**, and **second endings**. This makes the music easier to read and takes less space. **Sing** the song and follow the directions on the music.

En roulant ma boule

As I Roll My Ball

CD 4:26

French Canadian Folk Song

French: En rou-lant ma bou - le rou-lant, En rou-lant ma bou - le,
Pronunciation: ã ɾu lã ma bu lə ɾu lã ã ɾu lã ma bu lə
English: En rou-lant ma bou - le rou-lant, En rou-lant ma bou - le,

bou - le, Der - riér' chez nous, ya - t'un é - tang, En rou-lant ma
bu lə de ɾyeɾ she nu ya tœ e tã ã ɾu lã ma
bou - le. Be - hind our house there is a pond. En rou-lant ma

100

Listen to "En roulant ma boule." Sing the pitch syllables of the Playalong as you listen.

Play the notes through the second ending on a pitched instrument.

do   la₁   so₁

Playalong

do   so₁   la₁   so₁   do   so₁   la₁   do

bou	-	le,	Der	-	bou	-	le,	Trois	beaux	ca	-	nards	s'en
bu		lə	de		bu		lə	trwa	bo	ka		nar	sã
bou	-	le.	Be	-	bou	-	le.	Three	pret	-	ty	ducks	are

vont	baign-ant,	Rou	-	li,	rou-lant,	ma	bou - le	rou-lant,
võ	bɛ	hã	ɾu	li	ɾu	lã	ma	bu	lə	ɾu	lã
bath - ing	there. Rou	-	li,	rou-lant,	ma	bou - le	rou-lant.

En	rou-lant	ma	bou-le	rou-lant,	En	rou-lant	ma	bou	-	le.
ã	ɾu	lã	ma	bu	lə	ɾu	lã	ã	ɾu	lã	ma	bu	lə
En	rou-lant	ma	bou-le	rou-lant,	En	rou-lant	ma	bou	-	le.

Traditions Near and Far

CONCEPT
BACKGROUND
SKILLS
LISTEN, SING, DESCRIBE
LINKS
SOCIAL STUDIES, CULTURES, READING

Global Voices

"Afrakakraba" is a game song from Ghana, a country in West Africa. It is a singing game about comforting a crying baby. **Listen** to the song.

 LISTENING CD 5:1

Afrakakraba   Akan Folk Song from Ghana

Afrakakraba afrakakraba afrakakraba kotuwim
A little child sits in the sun crying all day.

Afra chawuhu chawuhu chawuhu
Child, turn around

Afra kofa wudofu
And go to your loved one.

drums from Ghana

MAP

UNITED STATES

GHANA

Ghanaian art objects

In the game for "Afrakakraba," there are no winners or losers. Everyone gets a turn!

Stories and Games

This story has been told for many years by the Ashanti people in Ghana. It is called "Anansi the Spider." It is the tale of how the world began. **Read** the story.

Anansi

Anansi the spider had six sons: See Trouble, Road Builder, River Drinker, Game Skinner, Stone Thrower, and Cushion. One day Anansi went a long way from home, got lost, and fell into trouble. Back at home, See Trouble cried "Father is in danger!" to the other sons. Then Road Builder built a road and said, "Follow me!" They came upon a river. "A fish has swallowed him!" one son cried. Then River Drinker took a big drink and swallowed all of the river. Game Skinner went and split open the fish. Then a falcon took Anansi up in the sky. Stone Thrower threw a stone at the falcon. Anansi fell from the sky as Cushion ran to help his father. Anansi landed softly. Later, Anansi wanted to reward his sons with a great globe of light that he found. He could not decide which son to give it to. He asked Nyame, the God of All Things, to hold the globe while he chose which son to give it to. He could not decide, so Nyame took the beautiful white light up into the sky. He keeps it there for all to see, even to this day.

—Ashanti Folk Tale

The game for the African American song, "Little Sally Walker," is almost the same as the game for "Afrakakraba."

Sing "Little Sally Walker" and play the game.

CD 5:2

African American Game

Lit - tle Sal - ly Walk - er sit - ting in a sauc - er

weep-ing and a - moan-ing o - ver all she's done._

Rise, Sal - ly, rise.___Wipe___ your weep-ing eyes. Put your

hands on your hips and let your back-bone slip.___

Swing it to the east.___ Swing it to the west.

Swing it to the ver - y one that you like best.___

LESSON
6

CONCEPT
FORM

SKILLS
LISTEN, MOVE, DESCRIBE

LINKS
CULTURES

Conduct Your Own Investigation!

Sometimes a **conductor** leads a band or choir as they perform music. The conductor makes sure that the beat is steady and that all the musicians use the same tempo. A conductor uses special patterns of arm movements to show the musicians how to perform the music. The **meter** of the music tells the conductor what arm pattern to use.

Listen to this African American song. If you were conducting this piece, what tempo would you choose?

Point to the meter in "Crawdad Song." There are two beats in the measure. This is the conducting pattern for every measure.

Practice this pattern. **Listen** to "Crawdad Song" and perform the conducting pattern.

When you sing, you need to take breaths. Where is the best place to take a breath?

Look at the music and find the phrases. Now sing the song. Take turns conducting the class as they sing the song.

Crawdad Song

CD 5:5

African American

1. You get a line, and I'll get a pole,__ hon-ey._____
2. Get up old__ man, you slept too__ late,__ hon-ey._____
3. Get up old__ wom-an you slept too__ late,__ hon-ey._____
4. A - long come a man with a sack on his back,__ hon-ey._____ A-
5. What you gon - na do when the lake goes_ dry,__ hon-ey._____

You get a line, and I'll get a pole,__ babe._____
Get up old__ man, you slept too__ late,__ babe._____
Get up old__ wom-an you slept too__ late,__ babe._____
long come a man with a sack on his back,__ babe._____ A-
What you gon - na do when the lake goes_ dry,___ babe?_____

You get a line, and I'll get a pole, and
Get up old__ man, you slept too__ late;_____
Get up old__ wom-an you slept too__ late;_____
long come a man with a sack on his back, pack-in'
What you gon - na do when the lake goes__ dry? Sit

we'll go down to the craw - dad hole,_____
last piece of craw - dad's__ on your plate,_____
craw - dad man done__ passed your gate,_____
all the craw - dads__ he can pack,_____
on the bank and watch the craw - dads die,_____

hon - ey,_____ su-gar ba - by, mine._____

Unit 3 Tunes, Tales, and Traditions

107

Lullaby Time

"Crawdad Song" is a fun song. "Duerme Negrito" is a very different type of song. It is a lullaby. Lullabies are sung to calm and soothe people to sleep. This song is in ⁴ meter. The conducting pattern for ⁴ looks like this:

Practice this pattern. **Listen** to "Duerme Negrito." When the percussion begins, try to conduct ⁴ or move to the beat.

 LISTENING CD 5:8

Duerme Negrito by Atahualpa Yupanqui
This lullaby is sung in Argentina. What do you find calm and soothing about it?

Meet the Musician

Mercedes Sosa (b. 1935) sings "Duerme Negrito." She was born in Tucuman, Argentina, and became one of the most important singers of Latin America. She sings about the struggles and dreams of people all over Latin America.

Atahualpa Yupanqui (1908–1992) wrote "Duerme Negrito," and was born in Buenos Aires, Argentina. He was a composer, guitarist, and singer. When he was young, he rode around Argentina on horseback learning the songs of the people. Later, he traveled throughout South America learning more songs and stories. He performed these songs all over the world.

LOG ON

Log on to **music.mmhschool.com** to learn more about Mercedes Sosa.

LESSON
7

CONCEPT
RHYTHM
SKILLS
LISTEN, CREATE,
PERFORM
LINKS
CULTURES,
DANCE,
LANGUAGE ARTS

Move to the Rhythm

When people sing, they often find ways to move, like in "Little Sally Walker." **Listen** to this song from Mexico, and look at the words while you listen. What is the song about? How could you move to this song?

MAP

UNITED STATES

MEXICO

The Sea

CD 5:9

Mexican Folk Song

Listen to the song again and create some ways to move. **Sing** the song and add the movements.

When you dance, you are moving your body to the music. Some music has its very own movements. The **samba**, from Brazil, has its own special movements. When people dance the samba, they are showing how much they enjoy the music!

 LISTENING   CD 5:13

Medley Polleritas   by M.J. Castilla, Julio Espinoza, Gustavo Leguizamón, and Raul Shaw Moreno

Listening Map for Medley Polleritas

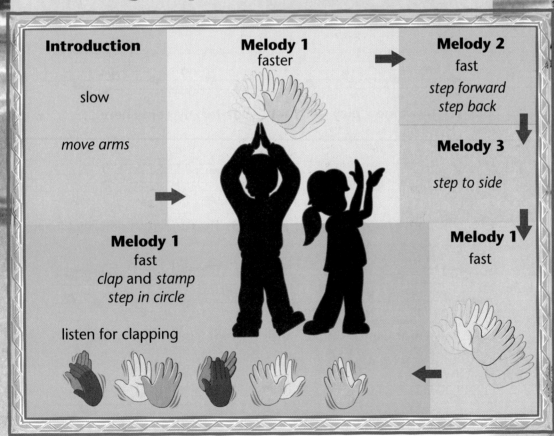

Introduction

slow

move arms

Melody 1
faster

Melody 1
fast
clap and *stamp*
step in circle

listen for clapping

Melody 2
fast
step forward
step back

Melody 3

step to side

Melody 1
fast

What kind of movements would go with the rhythm of this music? **Create** movements using different parts of your body.

Creating Movements

A person who creates a pattern of movements to go with music is called a **choreographer**. The **choreography** is the pattern of dance movements. When dancers learn the choreography to a song or dance, they practice the movements in the same order each time.

Sing this song. It is in two sections, AB. Then choreograph your own movements.

Butterfly Come Play with Me

CD 5:14

Words and Music by
Mary Ellen Pinzino

But-ter-fly come play with me. But-ter-fly come here.

But-ter-fly come play with me. But-ter-fly can you hear?

We will laugh and dance and sing and play. We will

fly through the air. We will laugh and dance and

sing and play and fly ev'-ry-where.

Create your own choreography for the A section. Decide the order to perform your movement choices.

Practice the choreography already created for the B section. Now perform the piece.

Perform your choreography for the class.

For B section only
Soprano Glockenspiel

Alto Xylophone

Alto Metallophone

(Repeat 7 times)

CONCEPT
MELODY
SKILLS
SING, READ, COMPOSE
LINKS
SOCIAL STUDIES

"Lukey's Boat" is a sea chantey from Newfoundland, Canada. Many sea chanteys come from the island of Newfoundland. **Listen** to "Lukey's Boat," and follow the music. The song uses low *so* and low *la*. Point to low *so* and low *la* in the music.

Sing the song.

CD 5:17

Newfoundland Folk Song

1. Oh, Lu - key's boat is paint - ed green, Ah -
2. Oh, Lu - key's boat got a fine fore cut-ty,

ha, me b'ys! Oh, Lu - key's boat is paint - ed green, the
Oh, Lu - key's boat got a fine fore cut-ty, and

fin - est boat you've ev - er seen. Ah - ha, me rid-dle - i - day!
ev' - ry seam is chinked with put-ty,

3. Oh, Lukey's boat got a high stopped jib,
   Ah-ha, me b'ys!
   Oh, Lukey's boat got a high stopped jib
   and a patent block to her foremast head,
   Ah-ha, me riddle-i-day!

4. Oh, Lukey's boat got cotton sails,
   A-ha, me b'ys!
   Oh, Lukey's boat got cotton sails
   and planks put on with galvanized nails,
   Ah-ha, me riddle-i-day!

5. Oh, Lukey's rolling out his grub,
   Ah-ha, me b'ys!
   Oh, Lukey's rolling out his grub
   a barrel, a bag, and a ten-pound tub,
   Ah-ha, me riddle-i-day!

6. Oh, Lukey he sailed down the shore,
   Ah-ha, me b'ys!
   Oh, Lukey he sailed down the shore
   To catch some fish from Labrador,
   Ah-ha, me riddle-i-day!

Some of these patterns also have low *so* and low *la* in them.

Sing these short patterns with pitch names.
Match them with the notated patterns below.

This school of fish swims in a pattern.

1 *do re do*　　**3** *do la so*

2 *mi re do*　　**4** *so la do*

Choose two patterns to put together.
Sing them one after the other.

Pitch of the Day

Clap the rhythm patterns.

Sing the patterns in the big colored fish. Pick a pattern from each fish. Put all three patterns together to create a larger pattern. Sing your pattern in the color order of the small fish in the box.

Spotlight Your Success!

REVIEW

1 Compare these two phrases from "Cumberland Gap." Choose the answer that best describes the two phrases.

   a. same length, same rhythm, different pitches

   b. same length, different rhythm, different pitches

   c. different length, different rhythm, different pitches

2 Which song does not have low *so* and low *la* in it?

   a. "Butterfly, Come Play with Me"

   b. "Gi'Me Elbow Room"

   c. "Lukey's Boat"

3 Which one of these is a conducting pattern?

   a.

   b.

   c. ostinato

READ AND LISTEN

CD 5:20

1 Which rhythm do you hear?

a.

b.

c.

d.

THINK!

1 How is a musical phrase in a song like a sentence in a paragraph?

2 How can you tell when one phrase ends and a new one starts?

3 **Write** about a song or dance from another country that you liked. Why did you like it?

CREATE AND PERFORM

1 **Create** a rhythm pattern in ² meter.

2 Your pattern should be 4 measures long.

3 Use ♩. and ♩♪ in your pattern.

4 End your pattern with ♩. ♪ 𝄾.

5 **Perform** your pattern on an unpitched instrument.

Meet the Musician
ON NATIONAL RADIO!

Barbara Vante
Age: 13
Instrument: Viola
Hometown: Boston, Massachusetts

Thirteen-year-old Barbara Vante has a wonderful way of describing the sound made by her favorite instrument. "The viola has a chocolaty creamy sound that is nice and melting and has flavor!" she says.

Before taking up the viola, Barbara played the violin, which she thinks has a "strawberry cream" sound. She likes the deep, rich sound of the viola more, though.

Barbara also prefers the viola's larger size. "The viola suits me because I have big fingers!" she explains. "I can grab it more easily than the violin."

 LISTENING   CD 5:21–22   **RECORDED INTERVIEW**

Concerto in B Minor, Second Movement (Andante ma non troppo)
by George Frideric Handel (Casadesus)

Listen to Barbara's performance and interview on the national radio program **From the Top.**

Spotlight on the Brass Quintet

Did You Know?

A brass quintet consists of five musicians: two trumpets, a French horn, a trombone, and a tuba.

The players in a brass quintet sit in a semicircle. Because there is no conductor to keep everyone together, they need to see each other to carry on their musical conversations.

Each instrument in a brass quintet plays its own separate part. At any time, each instrument may be called on to play the main melody or an accompanying role.

The brass quintet and the wind quintet have one instrument in common: the French horn.

 LISTENING CD 5:23–24

Volta from *Dances from Terpsichore*

by Michael Praetorius

Sonatine for Brass Quintet, First Movement (excerpt) by Eugène Bozza

Listen to these two pieces for brass quintet. In the piece by Praetorius, written over 400 years ago, the instruments sound like they are dancing. The more modern piece by Bozza is written for the same five instruments.

Music on the Go!

People are on the go everywhere you look! Some people are on their way to work. Some people are rushing to catch a plane to a faraway place. Some people just want to enjoy the sunshine! Where do you have to go today? Whether you are off to look for adventure across the globe or across the street, music can go right along with you!

Coming Attractions

Sing songs in canon.

Hear and learn about an ancient Chinese instrument.

Create your own rhythm conversation.

"Movin' Right Along" is a song from *The Muppet Movie.* It has two sections, which we call A and B. The words and melodies in the A and B sections are different. **Sing** the song and see where the A and B sections are.

Movin' Right Along

from *The Muppet Movie*

CD 6:1

Words and Music by
Paul Williams and Kenneth L. Ascher

A

C   F7

1. Mov - in' right a - long_ in search of good times and good_ news, with
2. Mov - in' right a - long,_ we found a   life   on the high - way, and

D7   E

good friends, you can't_ lose,   this could be - come a hab - it.
your   way   is my__ way,   so trust my nav - i - ga - tion.

C   F7

Op - por - tun - i - ty __ knocks once, let's reach out and grab_ it.   To -
Cal - i - for - nia, here_ we come; that pie in the sky__ land.

D7   F

geth - er we'll nab__ it.   We'll hitch - hike, bus, or yel - low cab_ it.
Palm trees and warm_ sand, though sad - ly we just left Rhode Is - land.

Travel Phrases

CONCEPT
FORM
SKILLS
LISTEN, COMPARE, IDENTIFY
LINKS
SOCIAL STUDIES

When you plan a trip, one of the things that you have to decide is how you will get where you want to go. There are many ways to get around. You can take a bus, a car, or a train. What other types of transportation can you think of?

Listen to "Stevedore's Song."
A *stevedore* is a worker who loads and unloads cargo from ships. Does the stevedore in this song enjoy his job?

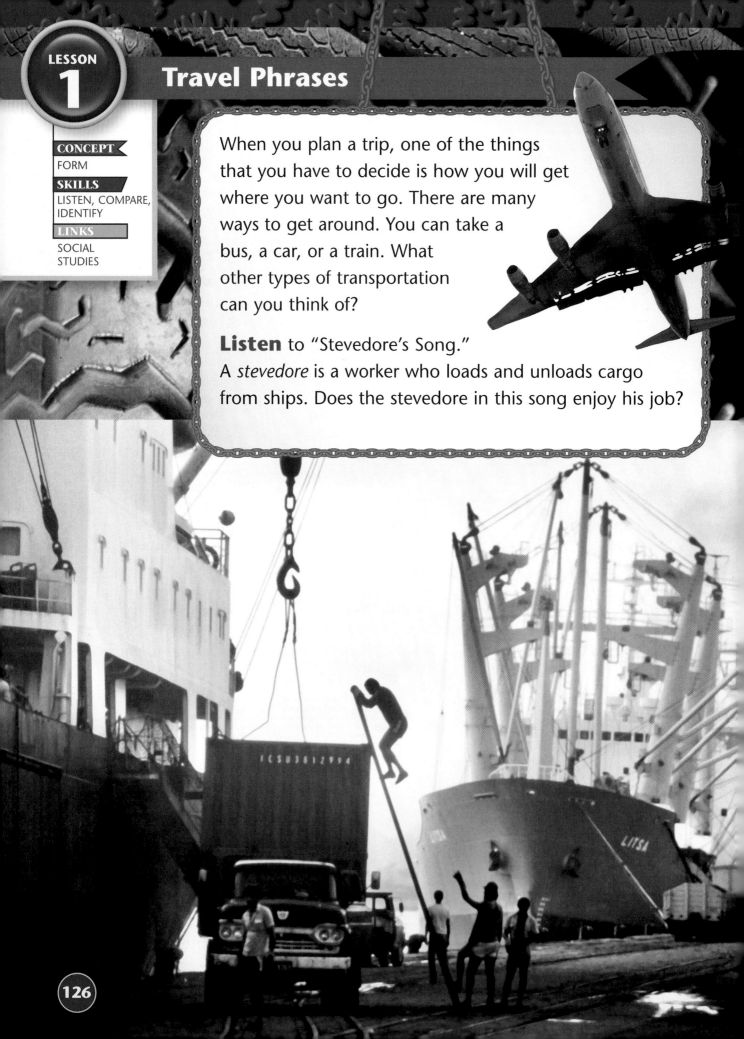

Sing "Stevedore's Song."

Stevedore's Song

CD 6:4

Calypso Melody

1. Get up in the morn-ing at the crack of dawn,
2. Wish I was a sail-or that put out to sea.
3. Then I get to think-ing of a sail-or's life:

work-ing in the sun the whole day long,
That's the kind of life, the life for me:
hard-ly ev-er sees his chil-dren and wife;

load-ing all the freight piled on the dock,
'stead of get-ting up at the crack of dawn,
when I'm load-ing ships down at the dock,

might-y glad to quit at five o'-clock.
work-ing in the sun the whole day long.
home for sup-per-time at six o'-clock.

"Stevedore's Song" has four short phrases in each verse.
Trace the phrases in the air with your finger as you sing the song.

Are the phrases the same or different?

Spinning a Phrase

"Spinning Song," by A. Ellmenreich, is about the motion of a spinning wheel. A spinning wheel was used many years ago to make yarn or thread. Tapping the treadle (foot pedal) with a steady beat kept the wheel turning.

 LISTENING CD 6:7

Spinning Song by A. Ellmenreich

The A section of "Spinning Song" has four short phrases. Some of the phrases are **identical**, or exactly the same. Some are described as **similar**, because they begin the same but end differently.

Listen for the similar and identical phrases in the A section of "Spinning Song."

Listening Map for Spinning Song

Here is another song about something else a-turnin'!
Listen to the four phrases in this song.

CD 6:9

African American Folk Song

There's a Little Wheel A-Turnin' in My Heart

There's a lit-tle wheel a-turn-in' in my heart. There's a
lit-tle wheel a-turn-in' in my heart. In my heart,___ in my
heart,___ there's a lit-tle wheel a-turn-in' in my heart.

Sing and pat the rhythm of each
of these pairs of phrases from
"There's a Little Wheel A-Turnin' in
My Heart." Then point to the word
to the right that describes them:

- Phrases 1 and 2
- Phrases 3 and 4
- Phrases 2 and 4
- Phrases 1 and 3

Identical

Similar

Different

CONCEPT
RHYTHM

SKILLS
SING, IDENTIFY, PLAY

LINKS
FINE ARTS

Before cars were invented, people rode horses to get where they wanted to go. Sometimes a carriage called a buggy was attached to the horse. When the automobile was invented, it was sometimes called a horseless carriage. Have you ever been on a buggy ride? Listen to "Riding in the Buggy" while you look at the picture of the horse-drawn buggies.

Art Gallery

Deep Snow, by Grandma Moses
The woman who painted this painting was called "Grandma" becase she lived until she was 101 years old!

Sing the song while patting the beat on your lap.

Riding in the Buggy

CD 6:12

Western Play-Party Song

Verse

Rid-ing in the bug-gy Miss Mar-y Jane, Miss Mar-y Jane, Miss Mar-y Jane, Rid-ing in the bug-gy Miss Mar-y Jane, I'm a long way from home.

Refrain

Who mourns for me, Who mourns for me, Who mourns for me, my dar-ling, who mourns for me?

Ostinato is the Italian word for stubborn. In music, an ostinato is a pattern that repeats without changing.
Perform this ostinato as an accompaniment for "Riding in the Buggy."

Hop on in. Take a bug-gy ride!

Clap the rhythm as you speak the pattern. How many sounds occur on each of the four beats?

The Beat Goes On

"Polly Wolly Doodle" is from the southern part of the United States. The words *polly wolly doodle* are nonsense words. As you sing the song, listen to how many sounds are on each beat when you sing the words *polly wolly doodle all the.*

Polly Wolly Doodle

🔘 **CD 6:15**

Southern American

Verse

1. Oh, I went down South for to see my Sal,
2. Oh, my Sal she is a_____ maid-en fair,
3. Oh, a grass-hop-per sit-tin' on a rail-road track, singing
4. Oh, I went to bed, but it was-n't no use,
5. Be - hind the barn, down_ on my knees,

pol-ly-wol-ly-doo-dle all the day.

My_____ Sal, she is a
With_ curl - y eyes and
A_____ pick-in' his teeth with a
My_____ feet stuck out like a
I_____ thought I heard a

spunk - y gal,
laugh - ing hair,
car - pet tack, sing-ing pol - ly - wol - ly - doo - dle all the
chick - en roost,
chick - en sneeze,

132

Do the words *polly wolly doodle all the* have the same rhythm? How many sounds are there on each beat when you sing those words?

mi re do

Listen to "Polly Wolly Doodle."

Sing the pitch syllables of the playalong as you listen to the refrain.

Play the pitch syllables on a pitched instrument during the refrain.

Playalong

Round Goes the Windmill

CONCEPT
RHYTHM
SKILLS
SING, IDENTIFY, READ
LINKS
FINE ART, LANGUAGE ARTS

Windmills can still be seen today on hillsides in Europe, the United States, and South Africa. Windmills have been used for centuries to grind corn and wheat. Windmills can also produce electric power by pumping water. Today, many people are still interested in the history and beauty of these buildings.

Art Gallery

A *Field of Tulips in Holland,* by Claude Monet
Holland, also called The Netherlands, is famous for the tulip flower. The field in this painting is full of them.

When the wind blows, the turning sails of an old windmill make a sound that can be heard over and over. The words *tique tique taque* imitate that sound in this song. **Listen** to "I Hear the Windmill."

Sing the song. **Pat** the rhythm each time you hear *tique tique taque.*

J'entends le moulin

I Hear the Windmill

CD 6:18

French Canadian Folk Song

French: **J'en-tends le mou-lin, ti-que ti-que ta-que. J'en-tends le mou-lin,**

Pronunciation: ʒɑ̃ tɑ̃ lə mu lɛ̃ ti kə ti kə ta kə ʒɑ̃ tɑ̃ lə mu lɛ̃

English: **I hear the wind-mill, tee-kah tee-kah tack-ah. I hear the wind-mill,**

ta - que. J'en-tends le mou-lin, ti - que ti - que ta - que.

ta kə ʒɑ̃ tɑ̃ lə mu lɛ̃ ti kə ti kə ta kə

tack - ah. I hear the wind-mill, tee-kah tee-kah tack - ah.

J'en - tends le mou - lin, ta - que. Mon père a fait bâ -

ʒɑ̃ tɑ̃ lə mu lɛ̃ ta kə mɔ̃ pɛ ɾa fɛ ba

I hear the wind-mill, tack - ah. My fa-ther had a

tir mai - son, ti - que ti - que ti - que ta - que. J'en-tends le mou - lin,

tiɾ mɛ zɔ̃ ti kə ti kə ti kə ta kə ʒɑ̃ tɑ̃ lə mu lɛ̃

fine house built, tee-kah tee-kah tee-kah tack - ah. I hear the wind-mill,

ti - que ti - que ta - que. J'en - tends le mou - lin, ta - que.

ti kə ti kə ta kə ʒɑ̃ tɑ̃ lə mu lɛ̃ ta kə

tee-kah tee-kah tack - ah. I hear the wind-mill, tack - ah.

Unit 4 Music on the Go!

135

Wheels of Rhythm

In "J'entends le moulin," you hear four sounds on one beat when you sing the words *tique tique*.

ti – que   ti – que

In music, four sounds on one beat can look like this:

 or

These are called **sixteenth notes**.

Look at the melodic ostinato of "There's a Little Wheel A-Turnin' in My Heart" on the next page. **Identify** the beats with four sixteenth notes.

136

Sing this ostinato with "There's a Little Wheel A-Turnin' in My Heart" on p. 129.

CONCEPT
MELODY
SKILLS
LISTEN, SING, IDENTIFY
LINKS
READING, CULTURES

What better way is there to start the day than with a song? **Listen** to "Rise Up Singin'." Does the first leap in the melody go up or down?

Rise Up Singin'

CD 6:22

Words and Music by Mary Goetze

When I rise up sing - in' in the morn - in',

then I will be sing - in' all the day.

Sing - in' at my work and sing - in' at my play,

spread - in' joy to all a - long my way!

Do can be on any line or space of the staff. Sing the names of the pitches on this staff, beginning with *do*.

Sing the last phrase of "Rise Up Singin'" using pitch syllables.

so	so	so	so	mi	mi	re	re	do
Spread-in'	joy	to	all	a	- long	my	way!	

Now sing the pitch names for the melody of *When I rise up sing-in' in the mornin'*. Hum the pitch when you see the question mark.

so	so	?	?	la	la	so	so	mi	mi
When	I	rise	up	sing	- in'	in	the	morn	-in',

Is the ? pitch higher or lower than *la*?
This pitch is called **high *do***, or *do¹*.

Sing the song, and raise your hand in the air whenever you sing high *do*.

Do can be on different lines and spaces of the staff, but the order of pitches is always the same. The order of the pitches is shown on the pitch stairs.

Find high *do* on the pitch stairs.

do¹
la
so
mi
re
do
la,
so,

Playing Up the Scale

Songs that have melodies only containing the pitches *do*, *re*, *mi*, *so* and *la* are called **pentatonic** songs. The word *penta* is the Greek word for "five." Tonic is another word for "tone" or pitch.

Even if a song uses low *la*, low *so*, and high *do*, the song is still pentatonic if it uses only five pitch names (*do*, *re*, *mi*, *so*, and *la*).

Look at the music for "Rise Up Singin'." Is it a pentatonic song?

When all eight pitches are placed in order from *do* to *do*, it is a scale. A **scale** is a group of pitches in order from lowest to highest.

Sing or play the pitch syllables used in "Rise Up Singing" in order from the lowest to the highest.

You just performed a pentatonic scale!

D	E	F#		A	B		D
do	*re*	*mi*		*so*ₗ	*la*ₗ		*do*ᴵ

A **canon**, or **round**, is a song with a melody that can be sung by two or more groups, each starting at a different time. Listen to "Shalom Chaveyrim."

Sing the song in **unison**. To sing in unison means to sing the melody with others. There is only one part in unison singing. Now sing the song as a canon.

Shalom, My Friends

CD 6:25

Israeli Folk Song

Hebrew: שָׁ - לוֹם חַ - בֵ - רִים שָׁ - לוֹם חַ - בֵ - רִים שָׁ - לוֹם שָׁ -

Pronunciation: sha   lom   xa   ve   rim   sha   lom   xa   ve   rim   sha   lom   sha

English: **Sha - lom   my___friends, sha-lom,   my___ friends, sha-lom,   sha -**

לוֹם - שָׁ אוֹת - רַ - הִת - לְ אוֹת - רַ - הִת - לְ לוֹם - שָׁ לוֹם - שָׁ לוֹם

lom   lɛ   hit   ra   ot   lɛ   hit   ra   ot   sha   lom   sha   lom

lom. We'll meet a - gain, we'll meet a - gain, sha-lom, sha - lom.

CONCEPT
FORM

SKILLS
LISTEN, SING,
COMPARE

LINKS
CULTURES,
LANGUAGE ARTS,
SOCIAL STUDIES

Global Voices

In Norwegian folk music, singing and dancing go together. "Her kommer vennen min" is a folk song from Norway. There is also a dance that goes with the song. **Listen** to the song.

MAP

UNITED STATES

NORWAY

LISTENING   CD 6:29

Her kommer vennen min Norwegian folk song

This is a well-known folk song. It is performed throughout Norway by folk music groups.

Her kommer vennen min og her kommer jeg
Here comes my friend and here I come.

Tra la la, tra la la

Her kommer vennen min og her kommer jeg
Here comes my friend and here I come.

Tra la la, tra la la

Nei du så bukker jeg
You curtsy, then I will bow

Nei du så bukker jeg
You curtsy, then I will bow

Akta deg; du får meg
Watch out for me,

ellers tar jeg deg
or I will take you!

Art Gallery

Motive from the County of Nordland

Adelsteen Normann (1848–1918) often painted images of fjords. A fjord is a long and narrow strip of sea between tall, steep slopes.

Norwegian Memories

"Oleanna" is a Norwegian emigrant song. People from Norway who came to live in the United States sang this song. It brought back memories of Norway.

Sing "Oleanna." How many different sections are there? Are the sections the same or different?

OLEANNA

CD 6:30

Norwegian Emigrant Song
Words Adapted by Jerry Silverman

Verse

1. Oh, my fel - low coun - try - men, if you'd be - come a mil - lion - aire, just head for O - le - an - na, all your
2. Talk a - bout good things to eat, they've got them there, and that's no lie. Ap - ple stru - del, ap - ple dump - lings,
3. O - le - an - na, that's the place. That's the place for you and me, where they pay you to re - lax, and

Listen to this dance by Edvard Grieg.

 LISTENING CD 6:33

Norwegian Dance, Op. 35, No. 2 by Edvard Grieg

Edvard Grieg was a famous composer from Norway. Most of his music was based on familiar Norwegian folk songs.

How many times does the A section repeat? How is the A section different from the B section?

 Log on to **music.mmhschool.com** to learn more about Edvard Grieg.

fond - est dreams will all be there.
ap - ple sauce, and ap - ple pie.
when you sleep, it's doub - le fee.

Refrain

O - le, O - le - an - na, O - le, O - le - an - na,

O - le, O - le, O - le, O - le, O - le, O - le - an - na.

Melodies in Motion

CONCEPT
MELODY
SKILLS
SING, DESCRIBE, COMPARE
LINKS
CULTURES, LANGUAGE ARTS, SOCIAL STUDIES

"Jasmine Flower" is a folk song from China. It is about the beauty and lovely scent of the jasmine flower.
Sing "Jasmine Flower."

MAP
UNITED STATES   CHINA

Jasmine Flower

CD 7:1

Chinese Folk Song
Collected and Transcribed by Kathy Sorensen

do

Mandarin: 好 一 朵 美 麗 的 茉 莉 花 好 一 朵 美 麗 的
Pronunciation: hao yi dwɔmei li də mo li xwa hao yi dwɔmei li də
English: Oh, what a love - ly__ Jas - mine_ flow-er. Oh, what a love - ly__

茉 莉 花 芬 芳 美 麗 滿 枝 椏
mo li xwa fɛn fang mei li man ʒɛ ya
Jas - mine_ flow-er. El - e - gance and_ sweet per - fume.

又 香 又 白 人 人 誇
yo shyang yo bai rɛn rɛn kwa
Cher - ished_ flow-er all__ snow - y__ white.

Learn About the Erhu

The *erhu* is a two-stringed instrument from China. It has two strings and two tuning pegs at the top. It rests on the player's knee and is played with a bow. The *erhu* is one of the most popular folk instruments in China. It has been played for over one thousand years.

Playalong

讓 我 來 將 你 摘 下
rang wo lai jyang ni tsai shya
Let___ me___ gen - tly pick you___ now,

送 給 別 人 家
song gei byɛ rɛn jya
Send you___ to___ my___ love.

茉 莉 花 茉 莉 花
mo li xwa mo li xwa
Jas - mine flow-er, oh, Jas - mine___ flow-er.

THINK! **Describe**

the sound of the *erhu*.
How is the sound like
the sound of the violin?

Unit 4 Music on the Go! 147

Which Way Did It Go?

Melodies can move in four different ways:
by **repeating** the same pitch,

by moving in **steps** from one pitch to the very next higher or lower pitch,

by **skipping** from one pitch on a line to the very next higher or lower pitch on a line, or by skipping from one pitch on a space to the very next higher or lower pitch on a space,

or by **leaping**, higher or lower, by jumping over more than one pitch.

"Pay Me My Money Down" is a song from the Georgia Sea Islands. It is about workers who load cargo ships. The melody is made up of repeated notes, steps, and leaps. **Listen** to the song and sing the response each time it comes.

Sing the whole song on the next page.

Use what you have learned about repeated notes, steps, and leaps to point to each and identify them.

Pay Me My Money Down

CD 7:5

African American Work Song
from the Georgia Sea Islands
Collected and Adapted by Lydia A. Parrish

Verse

Call   C

1. I thought I heard the cap-tain say,
2. As soon as the boat was clear of the bar,
3. Well, I wish I was Mis-ter Ste-ven's son,

C *Response*   G7   *Call*

"Pay me my mon-ey down,"

To-mor-row is our
He knocked me down with the
Sit on the bank and

G7   *Response*   C

sail-ing day,
end of a spar,
watch the work done,

"Pay me my mon-ey down."

Refrain

C *All*   G7

"Pay me, oh, pay me, Pay me my mon-ey down,

G7   C

Pay me or go to jail, Pay me my mon-ey down."

Playin' on the Old Banjo

CONCEPT
RHYTHM
SKILLS
LISTEN,
COMPARE,
COMPOSE
LINKS
VISUAL ARTS

CD-ROM

Use *World Instruments* **CD-ROM** to learn more about North American instruments.

Folk songs are a way that people can tell family and friends about good times through music. Some folk songs tell stories. Some are just for fun! "Dinah" is an American folk song. You can hear a banjo playing in this song. A banjo has five strings that are strummed or plucked. **Listen** for the banjo in the song "Dinah." Does the song tell a story, or is it just for fun?

Del McCoury Band

Dinah

CD 7:8

Minstrel Song

No one in the house but Di - nah, Di - nah,

no one in the house I know, I know; no one in the house but

Di - nah, Di - nah, play-in' on the old ban - jo.

Look at the rhythm of "Dinah." Which measures in green and red have the same rhythm? Which measures in the green and red have different rhythms?

These two lines are a musical conversation. The green line is the question, and the red line is the answer. When you and a friend have a conversation, you ask each other questions and give each other answers. A good answer always has something to do with the question. An answer is also different from a question. It always comes after the question and usually feels like an ending.

 Art Gallery

The Banjo Lesson

This was painted by Henry Ossawa Tanner (1859–1937), an African American artist. It shows a man teaching his grandson how to play the banjo.

Rhythmic Conversations

Clap each of these rhythmic questions and then pat a rhythmic answer for it. Use part of the question in the answer, and remember to finish with a quarter note on the last measure of the answer.

Perform one of these question and answer pairs with a partner during the instrumental sections of "Dinah."

THINK! Would you call these questions and answers identical, similar, or different? Why?

The American song "Oh, Susanna" also uses the banjo. Does this song tell a story or is it just for fun? **Listen** for the banjo playing in the interlude. **Sing** the song.

Oh, Susanna

CD 7:11

Words and Music by Stephen Foster

Verse

1. I___ come from Al - a-bam-a with my ban-jo on my knee.
2. I___ had a dream the oth-er night, when ev' - ry-thing was still.

I'm__ going to Loui - si - an - a, my___ true love for to see.
I___thought I saw Su-san - na a-com-ing down the hill.

It___ rained all night the day I left, the weath-er it was dry,
The__ buck-wheat cake was in her mouth, the tear was in her eye.

The__ sun so hot I froze to death, Su - san-na, don't you cry.
Says__ I, "I'm com - ing from the South, Su - san-na, don't you cry."

Refrain

Oh, Su - san - na, oh, don't you cry for me.

I___ come from Al - a-bam-a with my ban-jo on my knee.

Rondo a Round

CONCEPT
FORM
SKILLS
LISTEN, IDENTIFY, CREATE
LINKS
FINE ARTS, CULTURES

You are on the move every day. You go to school. You play with friends. You have hobbies. No matter how far you go or how long you are gone, you can always come back to the place you call home.

A piece of music where the A section always returns is called a **rondo**. The sections in between are different. The name rondo comes from the French word rondeau, which means "to come back around." A rondo form looks like this: ABACA.

Listen to "Gypsy Rondo." How many times does the A section return?

LISTENING CD 7:14

Trio for Piano, Violin and Cello No. 39, Finale ("Gypsy Rondo")
by Franz Joseph Haydn

The form of this rondo is ABACA *Coda*. A short section added to the end of a song is called a **coda**. *Coda* is the Italian word for "tail."

THINK! If you added another contrasting section of music to this rondo, what letter would you use?

Meet the Musician

Franz Joseph Haydn (1732–1809) is considered the father of the symphony and the string quartet. He wrote so much music during his lifetime that some of it has never even been performed.

Sad to Say I'm on My Way

Even when you have had a lot of fun on a trip, there comes a time to say farewell. **Sing** "Jamaica Farewell."

MAP

UNITED STATES

JAMAICA

Jamaica Farewell

CD 7:17

Words and Music by Irving Burgie

Verse

1. Down the way where the nights are gay and the sun shines dail - y on the moun - tain - top, I took a trip on a sail - ing ship and when I reached Ja - mai - ca, I made a stop. But I'm

Refrain

sad to say I'm on my way. Won't be back for man - y a day. My heart is down, my head is

156

Spotlight Your Success!

REVIEW

1 Which song has high *do* in it?

    a. Riding in the Buggy **b.** J'entends le moulin   **c.** Dinah

2 Which pair of phrases below can be called similar?

a.

b.

c.

3 Which pair of phrases can be called identical?

4 How does a short musical phrase become an *ostinato*?

    a. The musical phrase stops and starts.

    b. The musical phrase repeats without changing.

    c. The musical phrase is heard only during the second verse.

READ AND LISTEN

CD 7:20

1 Which rhythm do you hear?

    a.   **c.**

    b.   **d.**

2 All of these pitch patterns begin on *so.*
Which pattern do you hear?

a.

b.

c.

THINK!

1 How can you tell if a musical piece is a rondo?

2 When you look at a melody on the staff, how can you tell leaps from steps?

3 **Write** about the two canons you sang in this unit. What makes these songs canons?

CREATE AND PERFORM

1 **Create** rhythmic answers for the following questions. Form two groups to clap. **Perform** the questions and answers.

Meet the Musician
ON NATIONAL RADIO!

Name: Eoghan Conway   Age: 12
Instrument: Tin Whistle
Hometown: Somerville, Massachusetts

The tin whistle is a popular instrument in Ireland, where twelve-year-old Eoghan (pronounced Owen) Conway was born. He and his family moved to the United States when he was five.

Eoghan recently traveled back to Ireland to compete in a tin whistle competition. Young musicians from all over the world took part in the contest. Eoghan won first place!

"Many people think of the tin whistle as a toy, but it is a great instrument to learn music on," declares Eoghan. "It is also portable. When I go camping, I can bring my tin whistle and play around the campfire." Eoghan likes to play traditional Irish jigs and tap his feet along with the music.

 LISTENING CD 7:21–22 **RECORDED INTERVIEW**

The Gold Ring

Traditional Irish jig

Listen to Eoghan's performance and interview on the national radio program **From the Top**.

Spotlight on the Tuba

Did You Know?

The tuba was invented in Germany in 1865 for use in military bands.

Because of the tuba's big size, tuba players usually hold their instruments in their laps when they perform.

The marching band version of a tuba is designed to rest on the player's shoulders. The mouthpiece is in a different position to make it easier to play while marching.

The largest size tuba is eight feet tall with a tube length of 45 feet.

 LISTENING CD 7:23–24

Daniel in the Lion's Den (excerpt) by Francis McBeth

Sensemayá (excerpt)
by Silvestre Revueltas

Listen to the tuba solos in both of these orchestral pieces. The tuba plays an important role in Revueltas's colorful piece, inspired by the Native American music of Mexico.

UNIT 5

Sing a Wish, Dance a Dream

Wish upon a star and hope your dreams come true.

Night
Stars over snow,
   And in the west a planet
Swinging below a star—
   Look for a lovely thing and
   you will find it.
It is not far—
   It never will be far.

—*Sara Teasdale*

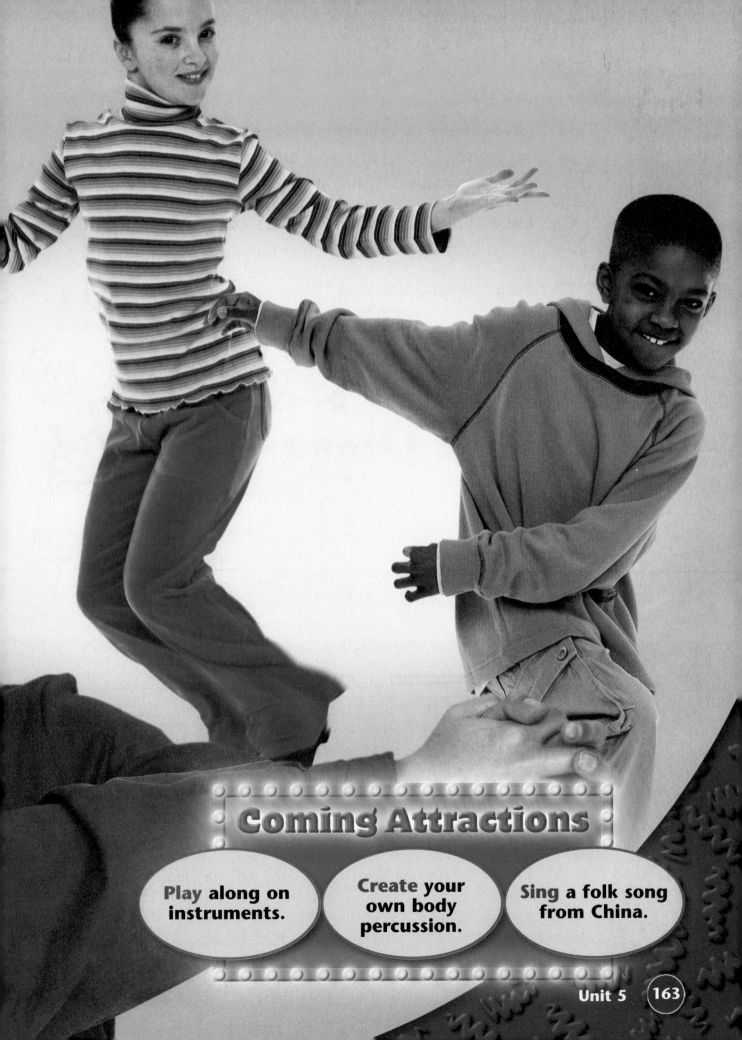

Coming Attractions

Play along on instruments.

Create your own body percussion.

Sing a folk song from China.

Have you ever seen a dog dig for a bone?
Sometimes a little hard work and determination are what
it takes to make a wish come true.

Listen to the ostinato in the first section of "Digga
Digga Dog" and speak the text quietly as you listen.

Sing "Digga Digga Dog."

Digga Digga Dog

from the movie *102 Dalmatians*

CD 7:25

Words and Music by Pamela Phillips Oland,
Mark Brymer, George Clinton, Jr.,
Garry M. Shider, and David L. Spradley

Dig - ga   dig - ga   dog,   dig - ga   dig - ga   dog.

Dig - ga   dig - ga   dog,   dig - ga   dig - ga   dog.

Dig - ga   dig - ga   dog,   dig - ga   dig - ga   dog.   Dog.

CONCEPT
RHYTHM
SKILLS
PERFORM, CREATE,
COMPARE
LINKS
CULTURES,
LANGUAGE ARTS

Sometimes you dream when you sleep. When you wake, your dreams can become hopes and wishes. What are your hopes and wishes? **Read** this poem about hope.

Hope

"Hope" is the thing with feathers—
That perches on the soul—
And sings the tune without the words—
And never stops–at all—

—*Emily Dickinson*

Pat the beat while you listen to the Spanish words in "Cielito lindo."

MAP

UNITED
STATES

MEXICO

Cielito lindo

 CD 7:28

Mexican Folk Song

Verse

Spanish: **De la Sie - rra Mo - re - na, Ci_e - li - to**
Pronunciation: de la sye ɾa mo ɾe na sye li to
English: **Com - ing down__ from dark moun - tains, Cie - li - to**

lin - do vile - nen ba - jan - do_____
lin do ßie nen ba xan do
lin - do, you____ **come to cheer us.**_____

There are three beats in each measure in "Cielito lindo," and a ♩ gets one beat. The meter of "Cielito lindo" is $\frac{3}{}$

Create your own 3-beat body percussion pattern to perform as you sing the refrain.

Night Music

Many pieces of music have been written about nighttime. One of the most famous was written by Wolfgang Amadeus Mozart.

Meet the Musician

Wolfgang Amadeus Mozart (1756–1791) and his older sister, Nannerl, were taught by their father when they were very young children. Wolfgang began composing music when he was only five years old! Their father took them on a tour of Europe. They played for royalty as well as the public in Germany, France, Belgium, England, and Switzerland.

 LISTENING CD 7:32

Eine Kleine Nachtmusik (Serenade No. 13 in G, K. 525) Minuet

by Wolfgang Amadeus Mozart

One of Mozart's best known pieces is *Eine Kleine Nachtmusik,* which means "A Little Night Music." It was written for a string orchestra. Mozart wrote this piece to entertain people in the evening.

This minuet is also in $\begin{smallmatrix}3\\•\end{smallmatrix}$ The conducting pattern for $\begin{smallmatrix}3\\•\end{smallmatrix}$ is .
Conduct as you listen.

Listening Map for Minuet from *Eine Kleine Nachtmusik*

LESSON
2

An Upbeat Day!

CONCEPT
RHYTHM
SKILLS
SING, LISTEN, ANALYZE
LINKS
CULTURES, GEOGRAPHY

The beats in "Cielito lindo" on pages 166 and 167 are grouped in threes. The first beat of each group is called the **downbeat**, or strong beat. The downbeat is usually accented. The last beat of each group is called the **upbeat**, or weak beat. The first word in "Cielito lindo" falls on a downbeat.

"Boll Weevil" is an American folk song that has its beats in groups of two. As you listen, **tap** on the cotton bolls to show two beats in each measure. **Tap** the first cotton boll on each downbeat.

Sing "Boll Weevil."

BOLL WEEVIL

MIDI

For another activity with "Boll Weevil," see *Spotlight on MIDI*.

CD 8:1

Southern Folk Song
Arranged by Mary Goetze

Verse

1. The Boll Wee-vil am a lit-tle black bug from
2. The first time I saw Boll Wee-vil,___ He was
3. The Boll Wee-vil to the farm-er said, "You'd
4. The mer-chant took__ half the cot-ton.___ The

Mex - i - co they say. Come all the way to Tex-as Just to
sit - tin' on the square. The next time I saw Boll Wee-vil, He had
bet-ter leave me a - lone. I done eat all your cot-ton, Now I'm
Boll Wee-vil took the rest. He on - ly left the farm-er Just a

Refrain

find a place to stay.
his whole fam' - ly there.   } Just a look-in' for a home.
start - in' on your corn."
sin - gle rag - ged vest.

Just a look - in' for a home.

Just a look - in' for a home.

Just a look-in' for a home.

Flagging the Upbeat Phrases

"Bella bimba" is an Italian song about a pretty girl dancing.

Pat, clap, and snap as you sing "Bella bimba."

MAP

Bella bimba

Italian Folk Song

CD 8:4

Pretty Girl

Refrain

Italian: Ma - co - me bal - li bel - la bim - ba, bel - la bim - ba, bel - la
Pronunciation: ma ko me bal li bɛl la bim ba bɛl la bim ba bɛl la
English: Now, see the pret-ty girl is danc-ing, she is danc-ing, she is

bim - ba, Ma co-me bal - li bel-la bim - ba, Co-me bal - li, bal - li ben!
bim ba ma ko me bal li bɛl la bim ba ke me bal li bal li bɛn
danc-ing, Now seethe pret-ty girl is danc-ing, she is danc-ing oh so well.

Verse

Guar - da che pas - sa La vi - la - ne - la,
gwaɾ da ke pas sa la vi la ne la
Watch as she pass - es the Vi - la - ne - la,

Go back to the beginning and sing to the end.
(Da Capo al Fine)

A - gi le e snel - la, Sa - ben bal - lor!
a ji le snɛl la sa bɛn bal loɾ
Grace - ful and slen - der, How she can dance!

"Bella bimba" has a verse and a refrain. The verse begins on the downbeat. The refrain begins on the last beat of a measure, so it begins on an upbeat.

Look at the accompaniment below. Does it begin on the upbeat or a downbeat?

Read the rhythm, then play the accompaniment on instruments during the verse of "Bella bimba":

LESSON

3

CONCEPT
RHYTHM
SKILLS
READ, WRITE,
ANALYZE
LINKS
CULTURES,
DANCE

Three to Get Ready!

"Tititorea" is the name given to Maori games played with rods or sticks. **Tap** the beat as you listen to "Tititorea."

Sing the song.

MAP

UNITED
STATES

NEW ZEALAND

Tititorea

Maori Stick Game

CD 8:8

New Zealand Folk Song
Collected and Transcribed by Kathy B. Sorensen

Maori: E hi – ne ho – ki mai ra.
Pronunciation: e hi ne ho ki maɪ ɾa

E pa – pa__ wai – a – ri ta – ku nei__ ma – hi,
e pa pa waɪ a ɾi ta ku neɪ ma hi

ta – ku nei__ ma – hi tu – ku roi – ma ta. Au
ta ku neɪ ma hi tu ku ɾɔɪ ma ta au

e au – e_____ ka – ma – te au,
e au e ka ma te au

Go back to the beginning and sing to the end.
(Da Capo al Fine)

E hi – ne ho – ki mai ra.
e hi ne ho ki maɪ ɾa

174

The Maori people are native New Zealanders. *Aotearoa* is the Maori name for their country. Elders, grandmothers, and grandfathers teach Tititorea to children. Stick games help them become strong, quick, and skillful with their hands.

Learn About the Tititorea Stick Game

The short sticks are called tititorea. They perform patterns in time with the beat. The patterns include tapping sticks on the floor or together, to the side or in front. They also flip the sticks from one end to the other. The patterns are performed by partners seated on the floor. They toss sticks back and forth with their partners.

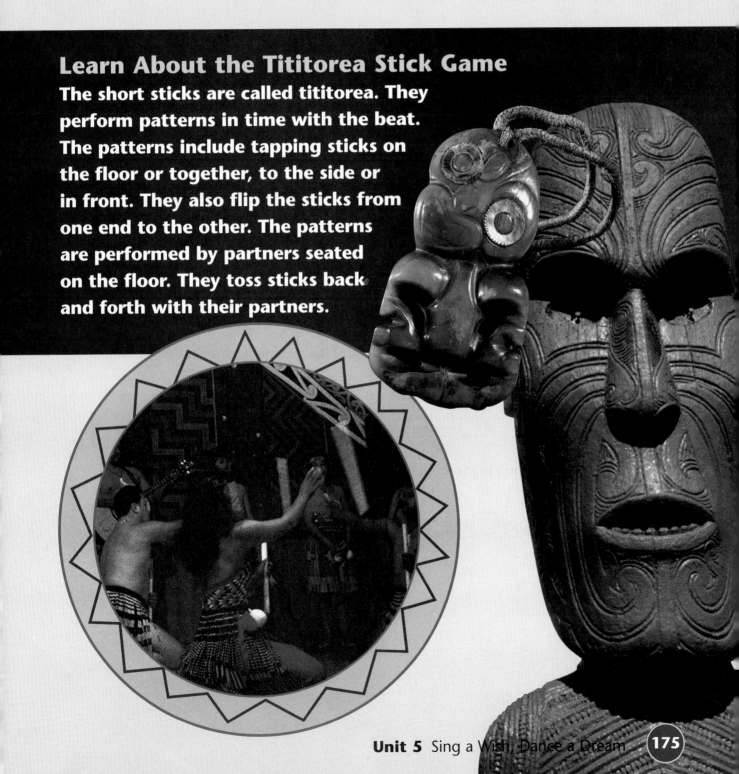

Staying on Track

Listen to this song about being far from home.
Tap the beat softly as you listen. **Sing** the song.

O, The Train's Off the Track

CD 8:12

Virginian Folk Song

1. O, the train's off the track, and I can't get it back, and I
2. If you say___ so___ I'll rail-road no more;___ I'll

can't get a let-ter to my home,
side-track my train and go___ home,

to my home, to my home, and I can't get a let-ter to my home.
go___ home, go___ home,___ I'll side-track my train and go___ home.

Perform a pat-pat-clap-snap pattern (♩♩♩♩) starting on the downbeat.

A sound that lasts one half note plus one quarter note is called a **dotted half note** (𝅗𝅥.).

Find the dotted half notes in the music of "O, The Train's Off the Track." **Sing** the song again, and raise your hand every time you sing a dotted half note (𝅗𝅥.). Now play along with the song.

What's the Whole Idea?

CONCEPT
RHYTHM
SKILLS
LISTEN, SING, CONDUCT
LINKS
SOCIAL STUDIES

LOG ON

Log on to **music.mmhschool.com** to learn more about J.S. Bach and his music.

The cello is the second largest stringed instrument in the orchestra. It is played with a bow, like the violin. The cello is so large that it rests on the floor. **Listen** for the cello in "Gigue" from *Suite No. 1 for Solo Cello in G Major* by Johann Sebastian Bach.

LISTENING CD 8:15

Gigue from Suite No. 1 for Cello *in G Majo*r

by J.S. Bach

Johann Sebastian Bach (1685–1750) was a German composer. He wrote many pieces for different instruments. This is from a group of pieces written especially for the cello.

Conductors help keep members of the orchestra or choir together by showing the meter of the music. The conducting patterns they use are based on the meter of the music.

Find the downbeat of both patterns. Find the upbeat of both patterns. What beat is the upbeat in $\frac{2}{4}$ meter?   In $\frac{3}{4}$ meter?

Conduct the 4-beat pattern below. Find the downbeat and the upbeat in this pattern.

Practice the 4-beat conducting pattern. Conduct the $\frac{4}{4}$ pattern as you listen to Gigue from Suite No. 1 for Cello again.

Freedom of Expression

A sound that lasts for four beats is called a **whole note** and is written like this: o

In $\frac{4}{4}$ meter, one whole note fills a whole measure. If a quarter rest equals one beat of silence, how many beats of silence would a **whole rest** (–) equal?

How is the whole rest – different from the half rest –?

Sing this African American song that contains whole notes.

How many whole notes are in this song?

Sing the song again. When you sing a whole note, draw a circle in the air during the four beats.

Clap this ostinato with the song. Where is the whole rest?

Play the ostinato on an unpitched instrument.

Playalong

THINK! How would you describe the feeling or mood of this song?

I'm gon-na walk, talk,— sing, shout,— hal-le-lu—— I got my

mind on free-dom. Walk, talk— sing, shout,— clap my hands and keep my

Go to the beginning and sing to the end
(Da Capo al Fine)

mind on free-dom. Walk, talk,— sing, shout,— clap my hands.

Would You Repeat That?

CONCEPT
FORM

SKILLS
SING, CREATE, PERFORM

LINKS
DANCE, VISUAL ARTS, CULTURES

When you make a wish or daydream about something you would like to do, you may picture it in your mind. **Listen** to this song about an imaginary toy. Try to imagine how the toy moves.

Sing "The Marvelous Toy."

The Marvelous Toy

CD 8:19

Words and Music by Tom Paxton

1. When I was just a wee lit-tle child full of health and joy, my
2. The first time that I picked it__ up I had a big sur-prise, for

fa - ther home - ward came one night, and gave to me a toy. A
right on it's bot-tom were two big but-tons that looked like big green eyes. I

won - der to be-hold it was, with man - y col - ors bright, and the
first pushed one and then the oth-er, and then I twist-ed its lid, and__

mo - ment I laid eyes on it, it be - came my heart's de - light.
when I set it down a - gain__ here is what it did:

Think of a 4-beat movement ostinato to show how the marvelous toy might move. **Perform** your movement ostinato when you sing the refrain.

Keeping the Baby Happy ...

by Rube Goldberg

How do you think the invention in the picture might work? What sounds might it make? **Rube Goldberg** (1883–1970) was an American cartoonist who drew funny inventions with many moving parts. Some of his cartoon creations might be like the toy in the song "The Marvelous Toy."

Refrain

It went 'zip' when it moved, and 'bop' when it stopped, and 'whirr' when it stood still. I nev-er knew just what it was, and I guess I nev-er will.

Unit 5 Sing a Wish, Dance a Dream

183

Playing with Ostinato

Minahasa is a region in the province of North Sulawesi, in the Republic of Indonesia. Minahasans are the people who live on or come from the northern tip of the island of Sulawesi. "Wéané" is a lullaby. It is a song that the Minahasans sing to put their children to sleep.

Listen to the words of "Wéané."

MAP

UNITED STATES

INDONESIA

WÉANÉ

CD 8:22

Menadonese Lullaby

Minahasa: O i - nang ni ké - ké, ma - ngé wi - sa - ko?____
Pronunciation: o i na ni ke ke ma ngi wi sa ko
English: Mo - ther won't you give me just one lit - tle cake?____

Ma - ngé wa - ki wé - nang, tu mu - lus__ ba - lé - ké_____
ma ngi wa ki we nang tu mu lus ba le ko
Hush my dar - ling you shall have one af - ter__ you a - wake.__

Wé - a - né, wé - a - né, wé - a - né to - jo!_____
we a ni we a ni we a ni to yo
Wé - a - né, wé - a - né, go to sleep my sweet!__

Da - i mau si - a - pa ko - t - ré____ ma - ké - wé.
da i mo si a po ko ta re ma ki we
From the vil - lage I shall bring you some - thing__ nice to eat.

184

Play these ostinato patterns to accompany the verse of "Wéané." Listen to one another as you play together.

Pat ostinato 1 as you whisper the words:

Sleep,   sleep   lit - tle   one.

Practice ostinato 2 this way: Clap the rhythm of the first two measures; snap the rhythm of the last two measures.

Wish for some-thing nice.   Some-thing nice will come.

Play the ostinatos together as a class.

- Play ostinato 1 on metal instruments.
- Play the rhythms that you clapped in ostinato 2 on larger wood instruments.
- Play the rhythms that you snapped in ostinato 2 on smaller wood instruments.

LESSON 6

Searching for Pitches

While you sleep at night, a whole world of creatures comes alive. One such creature is the cricket. The German song "Night Song" is about the nighttime song of the cricket. The melody has only three pitches. **Sing** the song.

German Lullaby

CD 8:26

All through the night, The moon is sil - ver bright,

Crick - et sings his ti - ny song. Sings it through the

whole night long. All through the night.

Pitches can be read with pitch syllables such as *do*, *re*, and *mi*. They can also be read using their letter names.

The letter names for the pitches on the staff above are G, A, and B. The **treble clef** (𝄞) at the beginning of a staff is sometimes called the **G clef**. It circles the second line to tell you that it is G.

Sing the melody of "Night Song" using the letter names of the pitches. **Play** the music below.

Name the Notes

This song, "Little Boy of the Sheep," is from the Hebrides Islands off the coast of Scotland. Sheep are raised by many people who live there. The song is about the things a shepherd might do to pass the time while guarding sheep in the fields. **Sing** the song.

Look at the tinted pitches. Sing "Little Boy of the Sheep." Use pitch names in place of the words on the tinted pitches.

The bagpipes are ancient instruments still played today. **Play** this rhythm with "Little Boy of the Sheep."

Bagpipe players at the Cowal Highland Games in Dunoon, Scotland

Playalong

LESSON
7

CONCEPT
TEXTURE
SKILLS
SING, IDENTIFY, PERFORM
LINKS
CULTURES, VISUAL ARTS

Wish for a Fish!

"Wang Ü Ger" is a Chinese fishing song. People often have to work together on a fishing boat to carry out tasks such as pulling ropes and nets. They all have to pull at the same speed. To stay at the same speed, workers often sing songs in the same tempo.

Listen to the song and follow the English words. **Sing** the song. **Listen** to the pronunciation of the Chinese words. Practice saying the words.

Sing the song in Chinese and English.

MAP

UNITED STATES   CHINA

WANG Ü GER

Chinese Fishing Song

CD 8:32

Chinese Folk Song
Collected and Transcribed by Kathy B. Sorensen
English Version by MMH

	C		G7		C		
Mandarin:	白	浪	淘	淘	我	不	怕
Pronunciation:	bai	lang	tau	tau	wɔ	bu	pɑ
English:	Though	the	waves___	run___	high	and	deep,

	F	C	G7		C		
	掌	稳	舵	兒	往	前	划
	jɑng	wɛn	duɔ	ər	wang	chiɛn	hwɑ
	We	sail	on___	the___	course	we	keep.

When someone asks you to accompany them, they are asking you to go with them. Sometimes people sing the melody of songs alone. Other times they may sing the songs with instruments adding sounds to go with, or accompany, the song. An **accompaniment** is a musical background to a melody. Name a song you have sung in class that has an accompaniment.

Some songs, like "Wang Ü Ger," can be accompanied with **chords**. A chord is three or more pitches that sound together.

This Chinese fisherman on a bamboo boat uses trained birds to fish for him. ▶

	F			C	F	G 7	C
撒	網	下	水	到	魚		家
sa	wang	sia	shue	dau	yu		jia
Throw	**the**	**net___**	**and___**	**let**	**it**		**fall,**

G 7				C		
捕	條	小	魚	笑	哈	哈
bu	tiau	da	yü	siau	ha	ha
Catch	**the**	**big** -	**gest___**	**fish**	**of**	**all.**

Add a Little Harmony

"Blow, Ye Winds, Blow" is another song about the sea. The accompaniment for "Blow, Ye Winds, Blow" uses many different chords. When different pitches sound at the same time, they create **harmony**. Sing the song.

 CD 9:1

Massachusetts Sea Shanty

You must make me a fine Hol-land shirt. Blow, blow,
You must wash it in yon-der___ spring. Blow, blow,
You must dry it on yon-der___ thorn. Blow, blow,

blow ye winds_ blow. And not have in it a
blow ye winds_ blow. Where there's not a drop of___
blow ye winds_ blow. Where the sun nev-er

stitch of nee-dle-work. Blow ye winds that a-rise, blow, blow.
wa - ter___ in. Blow ye winds that a-rise, blow, blow.
yet___ shone_ on. Blow ye winds that a-rise, blow, blow.

Use a melody instrument to accompany "Blow, Ye Winds, Blow." **Play** these pitches as you sing the song. Listen to the harmony the accompaniment makes.

Playalong

D A G A A A G A D G A D D G A D

THINK! Name an instrument that can play three or more pitches at the same time to make chords.

LISTENING CD 9:33

American Salute by Morton Gould
This piece was written for orchestra.
It features many instruments you know.

Listen for harmony in *American Salute*.
Identify instruments you know in the recording.

Keeping Track of Rhythms

CONCEPT
RHYTHM
SKILLS
PERFORM,
READ, SING
LINKS
CULTURES,
DANCE

Find the name and the notes below that mean:

- One sound on a beat.
- Two sounds on a beat.
- Four sounds on a beat.
- One sound lasting two beats.
- One sound lasting four beats.

Perform each of the note values above using these words and sounds:

- quarter notes—Whisper *patch*.
- eighth notes—Say *pocket*.
- half notes—Say *where* with your voice, starting on a higher pitch and ending by sliding to a lower one.
- sixteenth notes—Say *puttin' puttin'*.

Practice performing these two ostinati using the words *patch, pocket, where,* and *puttin' puttin'*.

Sing this Southern American singing game.

The Paw Paw Patch

CD 9:4

Southern American Singing Game Song

1. Where, oh where, is dear lit - tle Nel - lie?
2. Come on boys, let's go and__ find her,
3. Pick-in' up paw paws, puttin' em in your pock - et,

Where, oh where, is dear lit - tle Nel - lie?
come on, boys, let's go and__ find her,
pick-in' up paw paws, puttin' em in your pock - et,

Where, oh where, is dear lit - tle Nel - lie?
come on, boys, let's go and__ find her,
pick-in' up paw paws, puttin' em in your pock - et,

'Way down yon - der in the paw - paw patch.

Sing the song again and perform the two paw paw patch ostinati.

Dancing Rhythms

People in Israel often dance while singing songs. When they dance, they put the rhythm in their bodies instead of speaking an ostinato as you did in "The Paw Paw Patch." **Sing** "Let's Go Dancing."

UNITED STATES

ISRAEL

CD 9:7

Translated by Moshe Jacobson

Let's go danc-ing ev - 'ry one.   Let's go danc-ing, join the fun.

Let's go danc-ing in a ring.   Let's go danc-ing as we sing.

Let's go danc-ing in a ring.   Let's go danc-ing as we sing, "Ya -

lel,_____ ya-lel - li_____ ya-lel, ya - lel_____ ya-lel - li."   (clap)

Let's go danc-ing ev - 'ry one.   Let's go danc-ing, join the fun.

Jerusalem, Israel

Let's go danc-ing in a ring. Let's go danc-ing as we sing.

Let's go danc-ing in a ring. Let's go danc-ing as we sing.

Spotlight Your Success!

REVIEW

① Which one of these melodies starts on a downbeat?

a.

b.

c.

READ AND LISTEN

CD 9:1

① Which rhythm do you hear?

a.

b.

c.

② Which rhythm do you hear?

a.

b.

c.

3 Which rhythm do you hear?

a. $\frac{3}{4}$ ♩ ♩ ♩ | ♩. ‖

b. $\frac{3}{4}$ ♩ ♩ ♩ | ♫ ♫ ♩ | ♩ ‖

c. $\frac{3}{4}$ ♩. | ♩ ♩ ♩ 𝄽 ‖

THINK!

1 Can one recorder play a chord? Can one guitar? Explain why.

2 How can you tell if the song you are listening to has beat groupings of three or four?

3 Describe one way to create harmony to accompany a melody.

4 Which of these instruments can play a whole note— wood block or triangle? Explain why.

5 **Write** about what the conductor's arm movement pattern shows the orchestra besides the tempo. How does this help the orchestra play well together?

CREATE AND PERFORM

Create a 4-measure ostinato for "Bella bimba." **Perform** it for the class while your teacher plays "Bella bimba" on an instrument.

Meet the Musician
ON NATIONAL RADIO!

Name: Heidi Gorton

Age: 17

Instrument: Harp

Hometown: Pittsburgh, Pennsylvania

It is not surprising that seventeen-year-old Heidi Gorton decided to play music. Her parents and grandparents are all professional musicians. She has been surrounded by music her whole life!

Heidi's mother is a harpist. "I used to listen to my mother playing, and I loved the sound," remembers Heidi. "I wanted to play harp, too."

Heidi's parents are members of an orchestra that performs around the world. Heidi joins her parents whenever they travel. "I've gone to Vienna, the Canary Islands, Japan, South America, and France," she says. Heidi feels really lucky to have visited so many different places.

LISTENING   CD 9:11–12   **RECORDED INTERVIEW**

Danse Profane by Claude Debussy

Listen to Heidi's performance and interview on the national radio program **From the Top**.

Careers

Gail Boyd wanted to be a lawyer since she was five years old. At twelve, she knew she'd choose entertainment law. Although Ms. Boyd has only recently begun studying the violin, she's always enjoyed the arts. When she'd heard, as a child, how famous singers like Florence Ballard of The Supremes had been cheated by record companies, Ms. Boyd decided she wanted to protect artists.

For thirteen years, Ms. Boyd has managed jazz artists' careers by helping them get performances, recordings, and fair contracts. She has represented the Clayton-Hamilton Jazz Orchestra, a dynamite big band, for over eight years.

"Absolutely the most rewarding part of my career," Ms. Boyd feels, "is helping to keep jazz alive. It's important to build jazz musicians' audiences and keep young people interested in this art form."

Spotlight on the Cymbal

Did You Know?

A cymbal is a thin, plate-shaped metal disk. It is held at the middle so the rest can vibrate freely.

Cymbals can be played individually with drumsticks or small brushes, or used as a pair and struck one against the other.

 LISTENING CD 9:13–14

March (excerpt) from *Love for Three Oranges Suite*
by Sergei Prokofiev

Overture from *La forza del destino*
by Giuseppe Verdi

Listen for the cymbals. A pair of crash cymbals struck against each other makes strong accents. The "whoosh" of the single brushed cymbal creates atmosphere.

Express Yourself!

Music can make you feel happy, and it can make you feel sad. Music can make you want to move your feet! When you share music, you share all the ways that music makes you feel.

Coming Attractions

Play a counting game in Spanish.

Explore the sounds your voice can make.

Create your own music!

The song "Three Little Birds" was composed by Bob Marley. He was a famous musician and songwriter from Jamaica. The style of this music is called reggae. Read the words to the song and then listen to the music. **Sing** the song.

MAP

UNITED STATES

JAMAICA

Three Little Birds

CD 9:15

Words and Music by Bob Marley

Don't wor-ry a - bout a thing,

'cause ev-'ry lit-tle thing gon-na be al - right.

Sing-in' don't wor-ry a - bout a thing,

'cause ev-'ry lit-tle thing gon-na be al-right.

Homeward Bound

CONCEPT
MELODY
SKILLS
MOVE, SING, READ
LINKS
CULTURES, DANCE, READING

In baseball, the runner on base always heads for home. In music, the melody always heads for home, too. This home in music is called the **tonal center**. Melodies often begin on the tonal center, move away from it, and then return. The tonal center is usually the last pitch of a melody.

"The Ballad of the Bedbugs and the Beetles" has an ending that sounds final, or complete, because the melody ends on the tonal center.

Sing this song about a very unusual baseball game.
Listen for the tonal center.

The Ballad of the Bedbugs and the Beetles

CD 9:18

Folk Rhyme
Melody by Carol King

I woke up Sun-day morn-ing and looked up-on the wall.

The bee-tles and the bed-bugs were play-in' a game of ball.

The score was two to noth-ing. The bee-tles were a-head.

The bed-bugs hit a hom-er and knocked me out of bed!

Choose a spot in the classroom to call your home base. As you sing "The Ballad of the Bedbugs and the Beetles," move away from your home base. Move back toward your home base as the melody returns to the tonal center on the last word of the song.

Here are the pitches in the G pentatonic scale.

Use the pitches from the G pentatonic scale to create a melody for the rhythm below. End your melody on G.

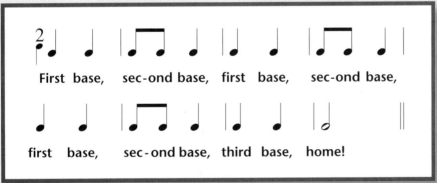

First base, sec-ond base, first base, sec-ond base,

first base, sec-ond base, third base, home!

Home at Last!

"Charlie" is a folk song from the British Isles about Bonnie Prince Charlie. Charlie is happy to be on his way home. The tonal center, or home tone, of "Charlie" is E. This song does not start on the tonal center.

Sing this song and listen for the tonal center.

Charlie

CD 9:21

Adapted from a
British Folk Song

Verse

Em   D   G

1. Step her to your weev'-ly wheat, and step her to your bar-ley,
2. O-ver and o-ver, ten times o-ver, Char-lie is a ro-ver;

C   G   Em   G

Step her to your weev'-ly wheat to bake a cake for Char-lie.
Take your part-ner by the hands and wring the dish-rag o-ver.

After you sing "Charlie," silently count to ten and then
hum the tonal center.

Refrain

O-ver the riv-er to feed my sheep, O-ver the riv-er, Char - lie!

O-ver the riv-er to feed my sheep, And mea-sure up my bar - ley!

Three to a Beat, a Mexican Treat

CONCEPT
RHYTHM
SKILLS
SING, MOVE, READ
LINKS
CULTURES, DANCE, READING

"Uno de enero" is a song from Mexico. It names the first seven months of the year. Look at the chart below. **Read** the first seven months, and count from one to seven in Spanish.

uno (one)	**enero** (January)
dos (two)	**febrea** (February)
tres (three)	**marzo** (March)
cuatro (four)	**abril** (April)
cinco (five)	**mayo** (May)
seis (six)	**junio** (June)
siete (seven)	**julio** (July)

Look at the music and find these Spanish words. **Listen** to the song and follow along with the music. **Sing** "Uno de enero."

MAP

UNITED STATES → MEXICO

UNO DE ENERO

The First of January

 CD 9:24

Mexican Folk Song

Spanish: U - no de e - ne - ro, dos de fe - bre - ra, tres de

Pronunciation: u no ðe ne ɾo ðos ðe fe βɾe ɾa tɾes ðe

English: First___ of Jan-u-a - ry, sec - ond of Feb-ru-a-ry, third of

mar - zo, cua-tro de_a - bril. Cin-co de ma - yo, seis de

maɾ so kwa tɾo ðea βɾil sing ko ðe ma yo seis ðe

March,___ fourth___ of A-pril, fifth___ of May,___ sixth of

210

La raspa Mexican folk dance

"La raspa" is a folk dance from Mexico. The melodies of "Uno de enero" and "La raspa" have three equal sounds on some beats. **Listen** to "La raspa" and raise your hand when you hear three equal sounds on one beat.

Tap this rhythm as you listen to the melody of "La raspa" again:

ju - nio, sie - te de ju - lio, San Fer - min. ¡A Pam-plo-na͜he-mos de
xu nyo sye te ðe xu lyo san fer min a pam plo ne mos ðe
June, __ sev-enth of Ju - ly, __ San Fer-min! To Pam-plo - na we must

ir con u - na me - dia, con u - na me - dia! ¡A Pam -
iɾ kon u na me ðya kon u na me ðya a pam
go, wear-ing a stock - ing, wear-ing a stock - ing. To Pam -

plo-na͜he-mos de ir con u - na me - dia y͜un cal - ce - tin!
plo ne mos ðe iɾ kon u na me ðya iun kal se tin
plo - na we must go, wear-ing a stock-ing, one "cal - ci - tin."

211

Take a Chance, Learn a Dance

The A section arm and foot movements for
"La raspa" imitate the motion of filing with a rasp.
A rasp is a file with small cutting teeth on the surface.

Practice these movements for "La raspa."

**Preparation for
A section:**

**Final form
for A section:**

**Preparation for
B section:**

**Final form for
B section:**

Begin the dance with your left foot. Each time you repeat
a 4-beat pattern, start on the opposite foot forward.

Perform the dance with a partner as you listen to "La raspa."

La Zandunga

Diego Rivera (1866–1957) was known mostly for his murals such as this one. The people in this painting are dancing in a traditional Mexican style.

CONCEPT
RHYTHM
SKILLS
LISTEN, SING, READ
LINKS
CULTURES, DANCE, READING

Dancing is a great way to express yourself! "El nido" is a popular *bailecito* (little dance) in Northern Argentina and Bolivia. **Listen** to the song while you tap the beat.

EL NIDO

The Nest

CD 9:29

Spanish: En el te - cho de mi ran - cho   Ba - jo el
Pronunciation: en el te cho ðe mi ɾan cho   βa xoel
English: In the roof - top of my cot - tage   live a

a - ler - o en un hue - co   Ba - jo el   a - ler - o en un
a leɾ oen un xwe ko   βa xoel   a leɾ oen un
pair_____ of nest - ing lin - nets,   live a   pair of nest - ing

hue - co.   Cuan - do em - pie - za a - ma - ne - cer   En mi rar -
xwe ko   kwan doem pye ɾa ma ne seɾ   en mi ɾar
lin - nets.   Lis - ten to the hap - py song.   I hope it

los me en_ tre - ten - go   Co - mo can - tan y re -
los men tɾe teng go   ko mo kan tan i ɾe
lasts the whole day long._   And my heart is filled with

to - zan Con a - le - gres a - le - te - os.   Tra la
to san kon a le gɾes a le te os   tɾa la
glad - ness to hear their mer - ry roun - de - lay._

Global Voices

Listen to this song about raising little chicks. It is from Azerbaijan, a mountainous country in western Asia. The Caucasus Mountains are located in Azerbaijan.

 LISTENING CD 10:1

MAP

UNITED STATES

AZERBAIJAN

Cip-cip cücələrim

by Gambar Huseynli and Tofig Mutallibov

Refrain

Cip-cip cücələrim,
Cheep-cheep, my chicks,

Cip-cip-cip-cip cücələrim,
Cheep-cheep, cheep-cheep, my chicks,

Mənim qəşəng cücələrim,
My beautiful chicks,

Tükü ipək cücələrim!
Chicks whose feathers are like silk!

215

Animals Go with Ostinatos

Find familiar rhythms in "One More River." This American folk song tells the story of Noah, who saved his family and many animals from a great flood.

One More River

CD 10:2

Nineteenth Century Song

Verse

Old No-ah, he built him-self an ark;
The an-i-mals went in one by one;
The an-i-mals went in two by two; } There's one more riv-er to
The an-i-mals went in three by three;
The an-i-mals went in four by four;

cross.
He built it out of hick-'rya bark;
The el-e-phant chew-ing a car-a-way bun;
The rhi-no-cer-os and the kang-a-roo; } There's
The bear, the bug, and the bum-ble-bee;
The hip-po-po-ta-mus stuck in the door;

Refrain

one more riv-er to cross. There's one more riv-er, And

that wide riv-er is Jor-dan, There's one more

riv-er, There's one more riv-er to cross._____

216

Clap this ostinato:

What   an   ark   he   built!

Perform this ostinato with pats and snaps:

snap

pat

Riv-er to cross, riv-er to cross, just   one   riv-er to cross.

Clap the first ostinato while you sing the verse of "One More River." **Perform** the second ostinato while you sing the refrain.

On the Move!

Home is a good place to return to after a long day. Melodies often return to a home tone at the end. **Listen** to "Bim Bom," and sing the first and last tone. Did the melody of "Bim Bom" return to the same pitch on which it started, its home tone?

The words to this song do not have any meaning, but they are fun to sing. **Sing** "Bim Bom."

BIM BOM

CD 10:5

Jewish Folk song

Clap the rhythm of the "Bim Bom" playalong.

Sing the pitch syllables of the playalong as you listen.

Play the pitch syllables on a pitched instrument.

Playalong

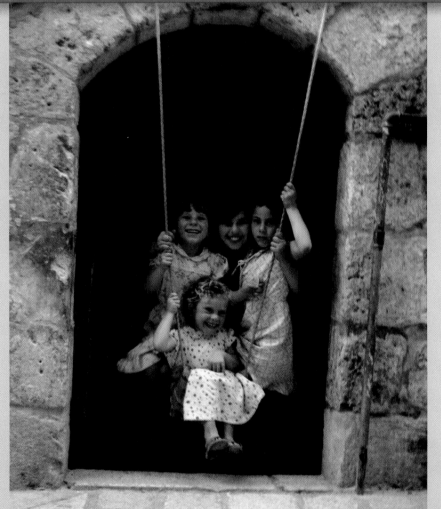

Tagging the Tonal Center

Look at music for "Moon and Me." Are the starting and ending pitches the same?

Sing the melody.

Moon and Me

CD 10:8

Words and Music by Bill Harley

Verse

1. Ev' - ry - bod - y else has closed their eyes,
2. I can see her shin - ing in the sky, through the
3. If there was a wish that I might try, I

it's as qui - et as can be. Ev' - ry - one will sleep un -
branch - es of the wil - low tree. Me here in my bed and
think I know what it would be. One night I'd have wings and

The End (Fine)

til sun - rise, ev' - ry - one but moon and me.
her so high, just us two, the moon and me.
then we'd fly to - geth - er, just the moon and me.

Sing the final tone of "Moon and Me." The tonal center, or home tone, of this melody is *do*.

In "Moon and Me," *do* is the tonal center, and in "Bim Bom," *la* is the tonal center. Discover the tonal center of this mystery tune. Begin by singing the melody using pitch syllables.

What is the name of this mystery tune?

THINK! Why do you think the tonal center is sometimes called the home tone?

CONCEPT
TEMPO
SKILLS
IDENTIFY,
DESCRIBE, SING
LINKS
READING, VISUAL
ARTS, HISTORY

Check Your Speed!

Look around you. Things are moving all around. What moves fast? What moves slow? How fast do you go?

Clap the beat as you say the nursery rhyme "Mary Had a Little Lamb." Change the speed of the words as you say the rhyme. How did the speed of the beat change?

Sometimes the tempo of a song changes. **Pat** the beat while you listen to "Draw a Bucket of Water." Did you hear and feel a tempo change?

Draw a Bucket of Water

CD 10:11

African American Play-Party Song

1.-4. Draw a buck-et of wa - ter For my on - ly daugh - ter.

There's { none in the bunch, we're all out the bunch,
one in the bunch, and three out the bunch,
two in the bunch, and two out the bunch,
three in the bunch, and one out the bunch,

(Four times)

You __ go un - der, sis - ter Sal - ly.

Sing the African American song "Draw a Bucket of Water."

THINK! How does the mood of the song change when the tempo changes?

The ⅞ sign is an **eighth rest**. It shows when there should be no sound on one eighth of a beat. (Remember that ♪ is an eighth note.) How many eighth rests (⅞) are in this song?

Frog in the buck-et and I can't get him out,

Frog in the buck-et and I can't get him out,

Frog in the buck-et and I can't get him out,

Frog in the buck-et and I can't get him out.

Russian to the Beat!

During the refrain of "Kalinka," the tempo gradually accelerates, or gets faster. The Italian musical term for this kind of tempo is **accelerando**.

Sing this Russian folk song.

KALINKA

CD 10:14

Little Snowball Bush

Russian Folk Song
English Words by MMH

Refrain

Em   B7

Russian: Ка   лин - ка, ка - лин - ка, ка - лин - ка мо -
Pronunciation: ka   lin ka ka lin ka ka lin ka mɔ
English: Ka - lin - ka, ka - lin - ka, ka - lin - ka____

Em   B7

я! В'са-ду я - го - да ма-лин - ка, ма - лин - ка мо -
ya vsa du ya gɔ da ma lin ka ma lin ka mɔ
mine! In the gar-den grows a ber - ry so sweet and____

1. Em   2. Em   End (Fine)   D

я! Ка - я. Ах,_____
ya ka ya ax
fine. Ka - fine. Oh,_____

Verse

G   D7   G   D7   G

Под__ сос - но - ю, под__ зе - лё - но - ю,
pɔd__ sɔs nɔ yu pɔd zɛ lyo nɔ yu
1. Un - der the__ pine tree, un - der the__ green tree,
2. Stur - dy_____ pine tree, shad-y ev - er - green tree,
3. Oh,__ my good__ friend, do not for - sake me,

224

Meet the Musician

Sergei Prokofiev (1891–1953) was born in Russia. He began composing when he was only five years old. He composed ballets, operas, symphonies, music for films, and pieces for piano.

 LISTENING CD 10:18

Troika by Sergei Prokofiev

Prokofiev wrote "Troika" to describe an exciting ride in a sleigh. A troika is a Russian sleigh pulled by three horses.

Спать	по - ло - жи - те___	вы	ме - ня.	Ах -
spat	pɔ ʒi tɛ	vɪ	mɛ nʲa	a
There	I'll___ lay___ me___ down	to	sleep.	Ah!
Do	not___ wake me with your	rust -	ling sound.	Ah!
Pro -	mise that al - ways you will	stand	by me!	Ah!

Ай___	лю - ли, лю - ли,	ай___	лю - ли,___
aɪ	lyu li lyu li	aɪ	lyu li
Ay,___	liu - li, liu - li,	ay,___	liu - li,___

Go back to 𝄋 and sing to the end
(D.S. al Fine)

Спать	по - ло - жи - те___	вы	ме - ня!	Ка -
spat	pɔ ʒi tɛ	vɪ	mɛ nʲa	ka
There	I'll___ lay___ me___ down	to	sleep.	*Ka* -
Do	not___ wake me with your	rust -	ling sound.	*Ka* -
Pro -	mise that al - ways you will	stand	by me!	*Ka* -

225

Smooth Move

CONCEPT
EXPRESSION

SKILLS
SING, PERFORM,
IDENTIFY

LINKS
CULTURES,
READING

There are many ways to add expression to music. Music can be smooth and connected. This is called **legato**. Music can also be short and choppy. This is called **staccato**. Performing music legato or staccato makes it more expressive. The song "Shoo Fly Pie and Apple Pan Dowdy" has lots of expression. **Sing** the song.

THINK! Do you think "Shoo Fly Pie and Apple Pan Dowdy" should be performed legato or staccato? Why?

Shoo Fly Pie and Apple Pan Dowdy

CD 10:19

Music by Guy Wood
Words by Sammy Gallop

Swing Rhythm

1., 3. Shoo fly pie___ and ap - ple pan dow - dy makes your
2. Shoo fly pie___ and ap - ple pan dow - dy makes the

eyes light up,___ your tum - my say, "How - dy."
sun come out___ when heav - ens are cloud - y. }

Shoo fly pie___ and ap - ple pan dow - dy,___ I

End (Fine)

nev - er get e - nough of that won - der - ful stuff.___

Ma-ma, when you bake,_ Ma-ma, I

don't want cake; Ma-ma, for my sake,_

Go back to the beginning and sing to the end
(Del Capo al Fine)

go to the ov - en___ and make some ev - er - lov - in'___ sh,

No Strings Attached

Staccato is shown by a dot above or below a note (♪♪♪).
Legato is marked by a flowing line over a phrase (♪♪♪).

Instruments in the string family are played with a bow. By using the bow, players can produce staccato and legato sounds. Sometimes string instruments are played by plucking the strings with the fingers. This produces a short sound called **pizzicato**.

Listen to "Holiday for Strings" by David Rose.

 LISTENING CD 10:22

Holiday for Strings by David Rose

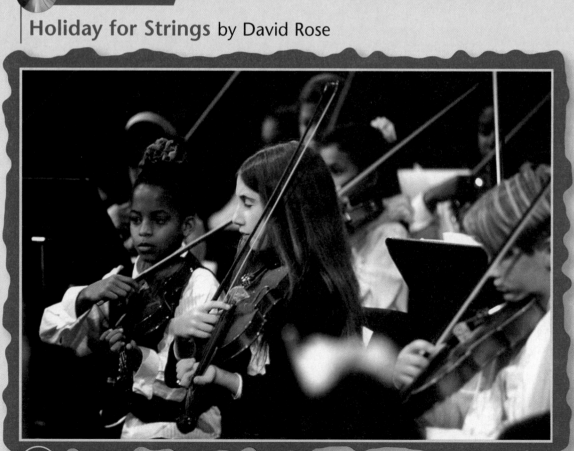

Holiday for Strings

In this music for strings, there are times when the strings play only pizzicato and other times when they play legato using bows. Work in groups to find a way to move when the strings play pizzicato, and a different way when they play legato sections of the music.

Listening Map for Holiday for Strings

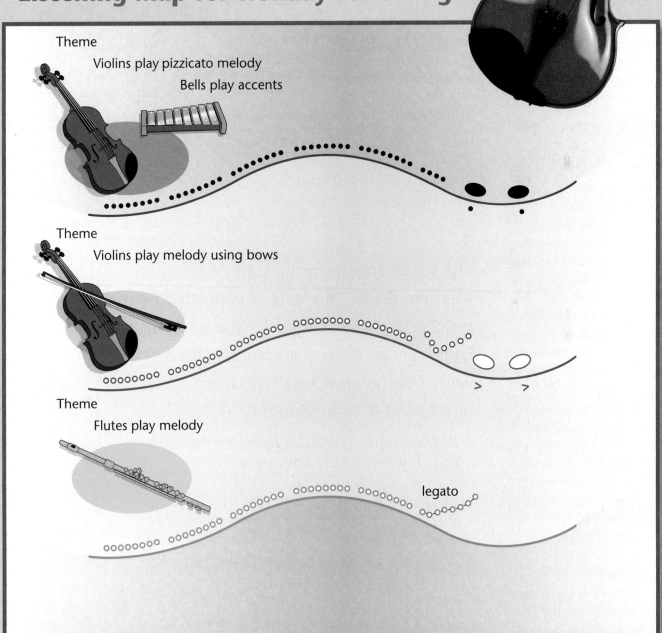

Theme
Violins play pizzicato melody
Bells play accents

Theme
Violins play melody using bows

Theme
Flutes play melody
legato

Singing Brazilian Style!

CONCEPT
FORM
SKILLS
LISTEN, PERFORM
LINKS
CULTURE, SOCIAL STUDIES

Global Voices

Some music from Brazil has its roots in folk music. Brazil has a rich tradition of folk music. "Pezinho" is a folk song from Brazil. **Listen** to the song.

MAP

UNITED STATES

BRAZIL

LOG ON
Log on to **music.mmhschool.com** to learn more about folk music from Brazil.

LISTENING CD 10:23

Pezinho

"Pezinho" has two sections, A and B. Each section has four phrases. Some phrases within the sections repeat.

The form of Pezinho is:

A: a b a b

B: c d c d'

The song came from the state of Rio Grande do Sul in southern Brazil. This state is populated by many *gauchos*. *Gauchos* originally worked in rural areas, handling cattle. They are like cowboys of the American west. *Gaucho* musicians and dancers take pride in their history and their rural roots.

Ai bota aqui, ai bota aqui o seu pezinho
Ay! Put your little feet here.

O seu pezinho bem juntinho com o meu
Put your little feet very close to mine.

Ai bota aqui, ai bota aqui o seu pezinho
Ay! Put your little feet here.

O seu pezinho bem juntinho com o meu
Put your little feet very close to mine.

E depois nào vá dizer, que você se arrependeu
And after, don't go and say that you have regrets.

Art Gallery

Bambini Giocando
by Cándido Portinari

Cándido Portinari is well loved in Brazil for his versions of the daily lives of ordinary people. He painted this in 1960, and the people of Brazil loved it so much that they used it on a stamp in 1978 for Brazilian National Day.

"Pezinho" is a children's song, or *cantiga*. *Cantigas* are sung in a circle. The children hold hands and do what the lyrics tell them, like stomp their feet, clap their hands, and wave a handkerchief.

Meet the Musician

Kleiton and Kledir are Brazilian brothers who have been playing together under that name since 1980. Kleiton and Kledir are famous for performing Brazilian songs, including Pezinho. Since they are from the southern part of Brazil, their music has very different rhythms than the samba. Their style of music is called Brazilian Gaucho.

Name That Form

"Limbo Rock" is a popular rock and roll song from the early 1960s. There is a dance that you can do with this song. All you need is a limbo stick!

Sing the song.

CD 10:24

Words and Musc by
Billy Strange and Jon Sheldon

1. Ev' - ry   lim - bo boy   and girl   all a -
(2.) spread your lim - bo feet,   then you
(3.) self   a   lim - bo girl.   Give that

round the lim - bo world,   gon - na do the Lim - bo Rock
move the lim - bo beat.   Lim - bo an - kle, lim - bo knee;
chick a lim - bo whirl.   There's a lim - bo moon_ a - bove,

all a - round the lim - bo clock.
bend back, like the lim - bo tree. { Jack be lim-bo. Jack_ be quick.
you will fall in lim - bo love. {

In music, sections are often called A and B, or verse and refrain. Inside the sections are smaller parts, called **phrases**. Phrases are sometimes labeled a, b, c, and d.

"Limbo Rock" has two sections, A and B. The A section has four phrases. What is the form of the A section of "Limbo Rock"?

Are any of the phrases in the B section identical or similar? What is the form of the B section of "Limbo Rock"?

Jack go un - der lim - bo stick. All a -

round the lim - bo clock, hey, let's do the Lim - bo Rock.

Spoken: "Limbo lower now, limbo lower now. How low can you go?"

2. First you
3. Get your

Spoken: "Don't move that limbo bar. You'll be a limbo star. How low can you go?"

Cook Up Your Own Rhythms!

CONCEPT
METER
SKILLS
READ, CREATE, PERFORM
LINKS
READING, CULTURES, VISUAL ARTS

A **limerick** is a special kind of poem that describes an event with a funny surprise ending. Limericks have word rhythms in $\frac{2}{8}$ meter with three sounds on many of the beats.

I raised a great hullabaloo
When I found a large mouse in my stew.
 Said the waiter, "Don't shout
 And wave it about,
Or the rest will be wanting one too."

? THINK! **Describe** how the words of the limerick fit with the meter of the body percussion accompaniment below.

As you say the limerick, **perform** this body percussion accompaniment with a partner. There are three motions: pat your legs, clap your hands, and tap. For "tap," you and your partner place your palms together.

With your partner, choose three of the 2-beat rhythms below and use them to create an 8-beat phrase.

Use at least one pattern that has three sounds on a beat.

End your phrase with a 𝅘𝅥. or a 𝄽· on Beat 8.

Use your composed rhythms to create an introduction and coda for a performance of "Hullaballoo" in $\frac{2}{4}$ meter.

Fun in Mexico

"La bamba" is a fun song to sing in Spanish. It is also a dance. If you go to a Mexican festival, you might sing and dance to "La bamba." **Sing** this song.

CD 10:27

Mexican Folk Song

C 7   F   B♭   C 7

Spanish: **1. Pa-ra bai-lar la bam-ba,   pa-ra bai-lar la**
Pronunciation: pɑ ɾɑ βai laɾ la bam ba   pa ɾa βai laɾ la
          (2.) cie - lo,   pa-ra su - bir al
             sye lo   pa ɾa su βir al

F   B♭   C 7   F

bam - ba se ne - ce - si-ta u - na po-ca de gra - cia,
bam ba se ne se si tau na po ka ðe gɾa sia
cie - lo se ne - ce - si-ta u-na es-ca-le-ra gran-de,
sye lo se ne se si tau naes ka le ɾa gran de

C 7   F   B♭   C 7   F   B♭

u - na po-ca de gra-cia y o-tra co - si-ta y a-rri-ba y a-rri-ba,
u na po ka ðe gɾa sia yo tra ko si ta ya ɾi βa ya ɾi βa
u-na es-ca-le-ra gran-de y o-tra chi-qui-ta y a-rri-ba y a-rri-ba,
u naes ka le ɾa gran de yo tra chi ki ta ya ɾi βa ya ɾi βa

C 7   F   B♭   C 7   F   B♭   C 7

y a-rri-ba y a-rri-ba y a-rri-ba i - ré, por ti se - ré, por ti se - ré,
i a ɾi βa ya ɾi βa ya ɾi βai ɾe por ti se ɾe por ti se ɾe

236

Spotlight Your Success!

REVIEW

1 Identify the tonal center of each of the melodies below:

a. *do*   **b.** *la*

2

a. *do*   **b.** *la*

3

a. *do*   **b.** *la*

READ AND LISTEN

CD 10:3

1 Which rhythm do you hear?

a.

b.

c.

2 Which rhythm do you hear?

a.

b.

c.

THINK!

1 Explain the meaning of the home tone of a melody.

2 Describe how you figure out if a song's tonal center is *do* or *la*.

3 Why do you think composers and performers use sudden and gradual changes in the tempo and dynamics in their music?

4 **Write** about how you should change your performance of a song if you see the words *staccato* or *legato* on the score.

CREATE AND PERFORM

Create your own melody and rhythm over 8 beats.

1 Use *so₁ la₁ do re mi so la*

2 Use ² for your meter signature.

3 Use ♩♪, ♫♩, ♩., and 𝄽 to create your rhythm pattern.

4 Decide whether your melody should end on the tonal center of *do* or *la*.

Perform your melody for the class.

Spotlight on
Music Reading

Spotlight on Music Reading

A Mi-Re-Do Song

Learn a *mi-re-do* song about the weather.
Find a place in the song that has no sound to a beat
(𝄽), one sound to a beat (♩), or two sounds to a beat
(♫). **Sing** the song with pitch syllables.

mi

re

do

Rain Is Falling Down

CD 11:1

Traditional English Song

Rain is fall - ing down! Rain is fall - ing down!

Pit - ter, pat - ter, pit - ter, pat - ter, Rain is fall - ing down!

CONCEPT
MELODY
SKILLS
SING, READ, PERFORM

Sing Steps and Skips

Melodies can
- move one step at a time.
- skip a step.
- stay on the same step.

Sing *mi re do* by steps, by skips, and by repeating.

Sing "Frog in the Meadow" and find where the music moves by steps, by skips, or stays the same.

CD 11:4

American Folk Song

Frog in the mea - dow, Can't get him out!

Take a lit - tle stick and Stir him a - bout!

What rhythms can you find in this song?

Perform this rhythm with the song.

Hide frog! Run a - way!

Music Reading 243

Play with Rhythms

Learn a Japanese song for jumping rope.
Find ♫ ♩ and 𝄾 in the song.
Read the rhythm of the first line then the whole song.

Honorable Bear

CD 11:7

Japanese Folk Song
English Version by
Marilyn Davidson and Kathy B. Sorensen

Japanese: く ま さん   く ま さん   ま わ れ み   ぎ
Pronunciation: ku ma san   ku ma san   ma wa ɾe mi   gi
English: **Ku - ma san,   ku - ma san,   turn your-self a - round.**

く ま さん   く ま さん   りょう て を つい て
ku ma san   ku ma san   ɾyo te wo tsui te
Ku - ma san,   ku - ma san,   hands up - on the ground.

く ま さん   く ま さん   か た あ し あ げ て
ku ma san   ku ma san   ka ta a shi a ge te
Ku - ma san,   ku - ma san,   hop with one foot in the air.

く ま さん   く ま さん   さ よう   な ら
ku ma san   ku ma san   sa you   na ɾa
Ku - ma san,   ku - ma san,   Sa - yo - na - ra.

Sing the song and hop with the beat.

CONCEPT
MELODY
SKILLS
READ, SING

Practice Reading Pitches

Learn about *do re mi*.

mi   do   mi   do   mi   do   mi

mi   mi mi   mi re do re   mi   re   do

Who's That Yonder?

CD 11:11

African American Spiritual

1. Who's   that   yon - der   dressed   in   red?

Must   be   the   chil - dren   that__   Mo - ses   led.

2. Who's that yonder dressed in white?
   Must be the children of the Israelite.

4. Who's that yonder dressed in black?
   Must be the hypocrites a-turnin' back.

3. Who's that yonder dressed in blue?
   Must be the children that are comin' through.

THINK!   Both lines of this song
are four measures long. How else are
they alike? How are they different?

UNIT
1 · READING

CONCEPT
MELODY
SKILLS
READ, SING

A *Do-Re-Mi* Tongue Twister

Find *do re mi* in this song.

Woodchuck

CD 11:14

Traditional Tongue Twister
Music by Marilyn Copeland Davidson

Faster each time

do

How much wood would a wood - chuck chuck

if a wood - chuck could chuck wood?

He would chuck, he would, as much as he could,

And chuck as much wood as a wood - chuck would

If a wood - chuck could chuck wood!

Sing another melody, this time with pitch syllables.

do re mi mi mi mi mi mi re re do

re re re do re mi mi mi

March Past of the Kitchen Utensils
from *The Wasps* by Ralph Vaughan Williams

This piece is from an opera called "The Wasps" that is based on a Greek comedy written about 2,500 years ago.

The first theme of this piece begins like the *do-re-mi* melody you just sang.

Listen to "March Past of the Kitchen Utensils" and follow the listening map. Raise a hand each time you hear the *do-re-mi* melody.

Listening Map for March Past of the Kitchen Utensils

Sing with an Added Pitch

You have been singing songs with *do re mi*. This song has another pitch. What is it?

do   do   re   re   mi   ?

Let Us Chase the Squirrel

CD 11:18

North Carolina Game Song

1. Let us chase the squir - rel,   Up the hick'-ry,   down the hick'-ry,
2. If you want to catch him,   Up the hick'-ry,   down the hick'-ry,

Let   us   chase the   squir - rel   Up   the   hick' - ry   tree!
If   you   want to   catch him,   Learn to climb a   tree!

Do, Re, Mi, So, and La

Learn to sing a *pentatonic,* or five-tone, song.
Sing *do re mi so la* then find those
pitches in "Coral."

 so   la

Coral

CD 11:21

American Folk Song

1.   O   sail - or   come a - shore.   What have you brought for me?
2. Did not take   it   from the ground, nor   pick   it   from   a   tree;

Red   cor - al,   white   cor - al,   cor - al from the   sea.
Lit-tle   in - sects made it   in   the   storm - y, storm - y   sea.

Find the half note ♩ in "Coral." Half notes are held
for two beats.
Practice singing the half note in "Coral."

More Pentatonic Melodies

Sing this pentatonic phrase with pitch syllables and letter names.

so so mi so la so mi mi re do

G G E G A G E E D C

Sing this song about a snowy winter day.

Frosty Weather

CD 11:24

Traditional

do

Frost - y weath - er, Snow - y weath - er,

When the wind blows, we all go to - geth - er.

Sing this ostinato with "Frosty Weather."

Cold wind

Imagine it is winter and you are outside at the end of a long, dark night. How would you feel when you saw the sun rise?

 LISTENING CD 11:27

Morning Mood from *Peer Gynt Suite No. 1,* Op. 46
by Edvard Grieg

"Morning Mood" is a piece for orchestra. The composer used a pentatonic melody to set the mood for a daybreak scene. The pitches of the first phrase are the same as those in "Frosty Weather."

Listen to "Morning Mood" and trace the shape of the melody.

Create your own morning melody by improvising with *do re mi so la.*

Sing a Pentatonic Song

Beep! Beep! Have fun learning a song about a car. There are three yellow patterns in this song. Which yellow melodic pattern in the song has repeated notes? Which pattern moves by steps? Which pattern moves by skips?

la
so
mi
re
do

I Have a Car

CD 11:28

American Camp Song

do

I have a car, it's made of tin.

No - bod - y knows what shape it's in.

It has four wheels and a rum - ble seat.

Hear us chug - ging down the street.

This car from the 1930s has a rumble seat.

Honk honk rat - tle rat - tle rat - tle crash beep beep.

Honk honk rat - tle rat - tle rat - tle crash beep beep.

Honk honk rat - tle rat - tle rat - tle crash beep beep.

Honk honk.

Name That Pitch

What is the mystery pitch in the pattern below?

mi   mi   do   ?   ?   do

Find that pitch in the song.

Old Mister Rabbit

CD 11:31

African American Folk Song

Old   Mis-ter   Rab-bit   you   got   a   might-y   hab-it   of

Jump-ing   in   my   gar-den   and   eat-ing   all   my   cab-bage.

Sing Low *La*

Learn another song about a rabbit.
Find the pitches in "See the Rabbit Running" on the pitch stairs.

See the Rabbit Running

CD 11:34

Hungarian Melody
Traditional English Words

See the rab - bit run - ning, from the fox who's cun - ning,

Fox is get - ting thin - ner, chas - ing down his din - ner.

An Added Pitch

Find *do* in this song.   *so*

Identify the new
pitch below *do*.

MAP

UNITED STATES

GUATEMALA

Vamos a la mar

CD 11:37

Let's Go to the Sea

Guatemalan Folk Song
English Version by MMH

do

F   C 7

Spanish:	Va -	mos	a	la	mar,	tum	tum,
English:	Let's	go	to	the	sea,	tum	tum,
Pronunciation:	ba	mos	a	la	maī	tum	tum

C 7   F

	a	co -	mer	pes -	ca -	do,	tum	tum;
	We	will	eat	some	fish -	es,	tum	tum;
	a	ko	meī	pes	ka	ðo	tum	tum

F   C 7

	bo -	ca	co -	lo -	ra -	da,	tum	tum,
	Bo -	ca	co -	lo -	ra -	da,	tum	tum,
	bo	ka	ko	lo	ɾa	ða	tum	tum

C 7   F

	fri -	ti -	to	y̦a -	sa -	do,	tum	tum.
	Fried	and	hot	and	spi -	cy,	tum	tum.
	fɾi	ti	to	ya	sa	ðo	tum	tum

Clap or play this pattern on
shells or wood instruments as
you sing the song again.

Shells

256

CONCEPT
RHYTHM

SKILLS
SING, READ,
CONDUCT

Conduct in Two

Practice measures 6 and 7 of the pattern below.
Read the whole pattern with pitch syllables.

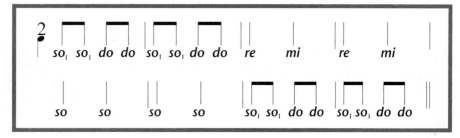

so₁ so₁ do do so₁ so₁ do do   re   mi   re   mi

so   so   so   so   so₁ so₁ do do so₁ so₁ do do

What is the meter of this song?
Conduct in two as you sing it.

1 2

Scotland's Burning

CD 11:41

Traditional Round

1
C   F   C   F

Scot - land's burn - ing,   Scot - land's burn - ing,

2
C   F   C   F

Look   out!   Look   out!

3
C   F   C   F

Fire!   fire!   fire!   fire!

4
C   F   C   F

Pour   on   wa - ter,   Pour   on   wa - ter.

Music Reading 257

CONCEPT
MELODY
SKILLS
READ, SING, MOVE

Sing with Low *La* and Low *So*

Move along with the words as you sing "Kreely Kranky." Find the pentatonic pitches in the song.

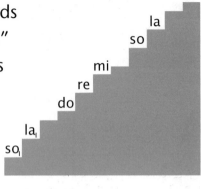

la
so
mi
re
do
la,
so,

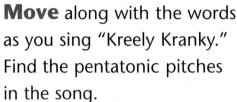

CD 11:44

American Dance Song

do

1. Kreel-y Krank-y is my song, Sing and dance it all day long,
2. Kreel-y Krank-y is my song, Sing and dance it all day long,
3. From my head down to my knee, Far-ther yet as you can see,

From my el-bow to my wrist, Here we give a dou-ble twist.
From my heel back to my toe, How much fur-ther can I go?
From my shoul-ders to my chest, In and out as you think best.

Sing this pattern and trace the melody.
Identify the pattern in the song.

do   do   do   do
         la   la
              so

do do do la, so, la, do

Keep the Beat in Four

Do you have a dog or a cat?
Sing this song.
Pat with the beat as you sing
it again.

Cat and Dog

CD 11:47

South Carolina Folk Song

1. Bought me a dog, bought me a cat.
2. Bought me a coat, bought me a hat.

They both fight but do not mind that.
They don't fit but do not mind that.

Hi ho, my dar - ling.

Find low *la* and low
so in the song.

A Pentatonic Song

Long ago, sailors sang songs like this to entertain themselves at sea.

Sing this pattern with pitch syllables.

Turn the Glasses Over

CD 11:50

Ⓐ
Verse

American Folk Song

I've been to Haar - lem, I've been to Do - ver,

I've trav - eled this wide world all o - ver,

O - ver, o - ver, three times o - ver,

Drink what you have to drink and turn the glass - es o - ver.

THINK! Count how many times you find the pattern above, or one like it, in the song.
How are the patterns the same?
How are some of them different?

The form of this song can be shown like this:

A   B

What is another name for the form of this song?
Look for clues in the song.

Equal and Unequal

♫ and ♩ get one beat in ⁴₄ meter.
In ²₄. meter, each of these rhythms gets one beat:

♩. 𝄽. ♫♫ ♫♪

The last of these rhythms is unequal: long-short.

Read, conduct, and compare these two poems.

Our Washing Machine

Our washing machine
 went whisity whirr
Whisity whisity whisity whirr
One day at noon it went whisity click
Whisity whisity whisity click
Click grr click grr click grr click
Call the repairman
Fix it . . . Quick!

—*Patricia Hubbell*

I woke up in the morning

I woke up in the morning
and I jumped out of bed
put some clothes on my body
and a hat on my head
took a leap to the kitchen
and I ate my toast
listened to the news
from coast to coast
looked out the window
to check the sun
ran out the door
to have some fun

—*Sonja Dunn*

Which of these patterns has equal rhythms and which has unequal?

²₄.		♩	♪	♩	♪	♩	♪	♩.	‖
		Click	grr,	click	grr,	click	grr, click.		

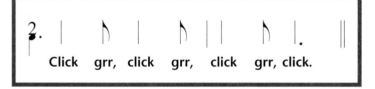

I woke up in the morn-ing and I jumped out of bed.

Say the third and fifth lines from "Our Washing Machine." These lines contain this rhythm: ♫♩♫♫

Playful Pizzicato from
Simple Symphony by Benjamin Britten

Simple Symphony is a piece for string orchestra.
In this movement, the string players play a
 pattern in ⅔ over and over.

Listen to this excerpt from the "Playful Pizzicato"
and softly say *whisity* while the orchestra plays.

Read this rhythm.
Learn a song in ⅔.

Chick - a - ma, Chick - a - ma, cran - ey crow.

Chicka-ma, Chicka-ma, Craney Crow

CD 11:54

British Folk Song

Chick - a - ma, chick - a - ma, cra - ney crow,

Went to the well to wash his toe. When he got there his

chick - en was gone. "What time, old fox?"

"One!"
"Two!"
"Three!"
"Four!"

Sixteenth Notes

Four sounds to a beat looks like this.

Pat and say these rhythms from "Golden Ring Around the Susan Girl."

Gold - en   ring a-round the   Su - san   girl.

All the way a-round our   Su - san   girl.

Golden Ring Around the Susan Girl

CD 11:57

American Folk Song

Gold-en ring a-round the Su-san girl, Gold-en ring a-round the Su-san girl,

Gold-en ring a-round the Su-san girl, All the way a-round our Su-san girl.

UNIT 4 READING

CONCEPT
RHYTHM

SKILLS
SING, LISTEN, PLAY

Play and Sing Sixteenth Notes

Pat this rhythm and then count how many times it is in the song. ♩♫♫

Chicken on the Fence Post

CD 12:1

Play-Party Song

Chick-en on the fence post, can't dance Jo - sey,

Chick - en on the fence post, can't dance Jo - sey,

Chick - en on the fence post, can't dance Jo - sey,

Hel - lo, Su - san Brown - y - o.

Say and pat the yellow patterns in "Chicken on the Fence Post."

LISTENING CD 11:60

Batuque by Oscar Lorenzo Fernández

Listen to this piece in ABA form from Brazil.
Play the yellow patterns as you listen.

Music Reading 265

Sixteenth Notes and High *Do*

This song is about the rhythm of a clock. What pitches and rhythms are at the end of the song?

Clocks

CD 12:4

Traditional

Big clocks mark time slow - ly, tick - tock, tick - tock,

small clocks mark time fast - er, tick - tock, tick - tock,

tick - tock, tick - tock, And the lit - tle watch - es mark time

tick - y - tock - y, tick - y - tock - y, tick - y - tock - y, tick - y - tock - y.

Sing a playground song with high *do*.

Circle 'Round the Zero

CD 12:7

Traditional African American Playground Game

Cir-cle 'round the ze-ro, Find your lov-in' ze-ro, Back, back ze-ro,

Side, side ze-ro, Front, front ze-ro, Tap your lov-in' ze-ro.

Find the sixteenth notes and high *do* in this game song.

One Potato, Two Potato

CD 12:10

Indiana Folk Song and Game
Collected by Marilyn Copeland Davidson

One po-ta-to, two po-ta-to, three po-ta-to, four.

Five po-ta-to, six po-ta-to, Roll them out the door. Hot po-ta-to!

Practice What You Know

Sing and play a game with this pentatonic song.
Sing it first with syllables then with the words.

Jingle at the Window

CD 12:13

Ohio Play-Party Song

Pass one win-dow, ti - de - o, Pass two win-dows, ti - de - o,

Pass three win-dows, ti - de - o, Jin-gle at the win-dows, ti - de - o.

Ti - de - o, ti - de - o, Jin-gle at the win-dows, ti - de - o.

Answer That Rhythm

Clap or play these rhythm patterns.

Play them as you sing the song.

CD 12:16

Words and Music by Carl Orff
English Translation by Doreen Hall

Ding dong dig-gy dig-gy dong, Dig-gy dig-gy ding the cat is gone!

Ding dong dig-gy dig-gy dong, Dig-gy dig-gy ding ding dong.

Create an answer rhythm for each pattern above.
Choose an instrument and play your answers.

Sing and Listen for High *Do*

Listen to this song. Raise a hand when you hear high *do*.
Find high *do* in the music.
Read and sing the song.

Play instruments with "Morning Bells."

Down and Up: *So Mi Do Mi So Do*[|]

This melody uses the same pitches as "Morning Bells."

Pat the rhythm of this pattern, first slow then fast.
Read the melody with pitch syllables.

Compare the direction of this melody with that of
"Morning Bells."

 LISTENING / CD 12:22

Galop of Sancho's Donkey from
Don Quixote by Georg Philipp Telemann

This music is part of a collection of pieces about Don
Quixote and his adventures with his pal, Sancho Panza.
It sounds as if Sancho's donkey
takes a few fast steps then a
few long steps.

Listen to "The Galop of
Sancho's Donkey" and raise a
hand each time you hear the
"Morning Bells" pitches going
down and up.

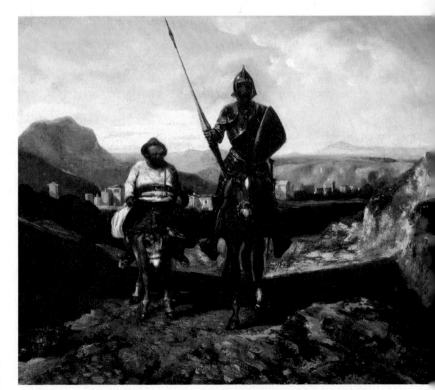

Don Quixote and his friend,
Sancho Panza

Play an Inner Hearing Game

Sing the song as you conduct the beats in two.
This song starts on which beat?

Smoke Goes Up the Chimney

CD 12:23

American Camp Song

do

First you push the damp-er in. Then you pull the damp-er out.

And the smoke goes up the chim-ney just the same.

Just the same, Just the same,

and the smoke goes up the chim-ney just the same.

Sing the song again. This time think the pitches of the yellow section instead of singing them out loud.
Clap or tap this ostinato with the song.

Start on a Pickup Note

The pickup in this song is an eighth note.

Remember that there are two eighth notes to a beat and ♪ ♪ = ♫ An ♪ gets one-half is a beat in ² meter.

Read and sing as you conduct this song in two.

I Lost the Farmer's Dairy Key

CD 12:26

African American Singing Game

1. I lost the farm-er's dair-y key, I'm in this la-dy's gar-den.
2. A brass key and a sil-ver lock, I'm in this la-dy's gar-den.

Do, do, let me out, I'm in this la-dy's gar-den.
Do, do, let me out, I'm in this la-dy's gar-den.

Eighth Notes and Eighth Rests

Clap this rhythm from the Mexican song "Que llueva."

eighth rests

An eighth rest (𝄾) gets one-half beat of silence in ² meter.

Que llueva

It's Raining

CD 12:29

Mexican Children's Game Song

Spanish: 1.–2. Que llue - va, que llue - va, la ra - na es-tá en la
Pronunciation: 1.–2. ke ywe βa ke ywe βa la ra naes taen la
English: 1.–2. It's rain - ing, it's rain - ing, the frog is in the

cue - va; los pa - ja - ri - tos can - tan, la lu - na se le -
kwe βa los pa xa ɾi tos kan tan la lu na se le
cave, And the par - a - keets are sing - ing, the sil - ver moon is

van - ta. ¡Que sí, que no!
βan ta ke si ke no
ris - ing. Oh, yes! Oh, no!

1. Que cai - ga un cha - pa - rrón.
   ke kai gaun cha pa ɾon
   The rain is fall - ing down.
2. Le can - ta el la - bra - dor.
   le kan tael la βɾa ðor
   The farm - er sings the song.

Whole Notes

Learn an Appalachian folk song about a robin.

Find the whole note. In 𝄴 meter, a whole note (o) is a sound that lasts four beats.

Death of the Robin

CD 12:33

Appalachian Folk Song

Dm

1. Who killed the ____ Ro - bin?
2. Who saw him ____ die? ____
3. Who dug his ____ grave? ____
4. Who let him ____ down? ____
5. Who preached at his fun - 'ral?

Gm   Dm

Who killed the ____ Ro - bin?
Who saw him ____ die? ____
Who dug his ____ grave? ____
Who let him ____ down? ____
Who preached at his fun - 'ral?

Dm   Gm

I, cried the spar-row, with my lit - tle bow and ar - row,
I, cried the fly, ____ with my lit - tle tin - y eye, ____
I, cried the crow, ____ with my lit - tle spade and hoe, ____
I, cried the crane, ____ with my lit - tle gold - en chain, ____
I, cried the lark, ____ with a song ____ and a harp, ____

Gm   Dm   Gm   Dm

It was I, Oh ____ it was I.

Dotted Half Notes and Whole Notes

Find the whole note in this Creole folk song.
There are also dotted half notes. In ♩ meter a ♩. is a sound
that lasts three beats.

Sweep, Sweep Away

CD 12:36

Creole Folk Song

Sweep, sweep, sweep a - way, Sweep the road of dreams,

Peo-ple say that, in the night, The tur-tle will talk, it seems.

The tur - tle will talk it seems.

Read this rhythm from the song.

Sweep, sweep, sweep a - way

Sweep the road of dreams,

Sing with Dotted Half Notes

Find the dotted half notes.

Sing "Little Tommy Tinker," first in unison then as a canon.

CD 12:39

Traditional

Little Tommy Tinker

Lit - tle Tom - my Tink - er sat up - on a clink - er, And he be - gan to cry, "Ma!___ Ma!"___ Poor lit - tle in - no - cent guy.

Rhythms in ³8 Meter

Read and sing this folk song from Tennessee.

My Horses Ain't Hungry

CD 12:42

Tennessee Folk Song

G   C   G

My hors-es ain't hun-gry, They won't eat your hay,

G   C   G

So I'll get on my po-ny, I'm go-ing a-way.

Sing and play this harmony part with the song.

Whoa, now! Whoa, now! Whoa, now! Whoa, now!

278

Rhythms of Celebration

Find the dotted half notes (𝅗𝅥.) in this African song celebrating the harvest.

Find the upbeat in the song.

Play this ostinato on drums or body percussion then play it with the song. Since "Dide" begins on an upbeat, so begin on the first full measure.

DIDE

CD 12:45

Ghanaian Children's Harvesting Song

Lobi: **Di - de   o   di - de   o   di - de   o,**
Pronunciation: di   dɛ   o   di   dɛ   o   di   dɛ   o

di - de   o   di - de   o - a   di - de   o
di   dɛ   o   di   dɛ   o - a   di   dɛ   o

A Song in 2.

Pat each of these rhythm patterns a few times.
Count how often each pattern is found in the song.

Old Roger

CD 12:49

British Children's Singing Game

1. Old Ro-ger is dead and he lies in his grave,
2. They plant-ed an ap-ple tree o-ver his head,
3. The ap-ples were ripe___ and read-y to drop,

Lies in his grave, lies in his grave.
o - ver his head, o - ver his head.
read - y to drop, read - y to drop.

Old Ro-ger is dead and he lies in his grave
They plant-ed an ap-ple tree o-ver his head
The ap-ples were ripe___ and read-y to drop

I ah I O I ay!

4. There came an east wind a blowing them off...
5. There came an old woman a pickin' them up...
6. Old Roger jumped up and gave her a knock...
7. Which made the old woman go hippety hop...

280

Military Music in ⅔

In ⅔ meter

𝅗𝅥. = 𝅘𝅥. 𝅘𝅥. = ♫♫♫

Find the dotted half notes (𝅗𝅥.) in "Taps."

CD 13:2

Traditional

do

Day is done, gone the sun, From the

lake, from the hills, from the sky; All is

well, safe - ly rest, God is nigh.____

LISTENING CD 13:1

Semper Fidelis by John Philip Sousa

John Philip Sousa wrote "Semper Fidelis" for the United States Marine Band.

Canons in $\frac{2}{4}$ Meter

When you sing in canon, you add texture to a song. **Sing** two canons in $\frac{2}{4}$ meter.

CD 13:5

Words by Mary Ann Hoberman
Music by Marilyn Davidson

1. Spi - ders sel - dom see too well.
2. Spi - der bod - ies are two - part.
3. Spi - ders al - ways have eight legs.

Spi - ders have no sense of smell.
Spi - der webs are works of art.
Spi - ders hatch straight out of eggs.

Spi - ders spin out silk - en threads.
Spi - ders don't have an - y wings.
Since all these facts are sure - ly so,

Spi - ders don't have se - pa - rate heads.
Spi - ders live on liv - ing things.
Spi - ders are not in - sects, no!

Find the *fermatas*, or holds, in this song.

Traditional Camp Song

Hel - lo! Hel - lo! Hel - lo! Hel - lo!

We are glad to meet you. We are glad to greet you!

Hel - lo! Hel - lo! Hel - lo! Hel - lo!

Tonal Centers

Find the tonal center in this song.

Cornstalk Fiddle and a Shoestring Bow

CD 13:13

Traditional

Verse

1. I made me a fid - dle and I made me a bow,
2. I tuned up my fid - dle and I went to a dance.

and I learned to play the fid - dle like Cot - ton Eye Joe.
___ I tried to make some mu - sic but I did - n't get a chance.

Refrain

Corn - stalk fid - dle and a shoe - string bow,

It's the ver - y best fid - dle in the coun - ty - o!

3. Cotton Eye Joe lived 'cross the creek.
   He learned to play the fiddle 'bout seven days a week.
   (Refrain)

4. I've made lots of fiddles and I've made lots of bows.
   But I never learned to fiddle like Cotton Eye Joe!
   (Refrain)

Refrain Countermelody

Corn - stalk fid - dle, And if that ain't fid - dl - in' then I don't know.

Follow the Melody, Listen for Form

LISTENING CD 13:16

Circus Music from *The Red Pony Suite*

by Aaron Copland

The piece is in three sections—like a 3-ring circus! The first and last sections are the same. What is the form?

Read and sing this pattern.

so mi re do la, so, mi, so, la, do re mi

Listen for this pattern in "Circus Music."
Follow the sections in the listening map.

Le cirque (The Circus), 1890-1891
by Georges Seurat

Listening Map for Circus Music

Sing with Ties

In 4/4 a whole note (𝅝) is held for four beats.

Find the whole notes in "Over My Head." How many do you see?
What do you notice about the whole notes?
How long are these sounds?

CD 13:17

African American Spiritual

O-ver my head, _____ I hear mu-sic in the air. _____

O-ver my head, _____ I hear mu-sic in the air. _____

O-ver my head, _____ I hear mu-sic in the air. _____

There must be a God some - where. _____

Sing this ostinato or play it on a pitched instrument. Begin the ostinato on the first full measure of the song.

286

CONCEPT
RHYTHM
SKILLS
READ, SING

Ties and Slurs

Read the pattern then sing the song.

Slur   Tie

do   Tramp - in' _____

CD 13:20

Swing Rhythm

African American Spiritual
Adapted by René Boyer-Alexander

Refrain

Call   F   *Response*   C   F

I'm tramp-in', ___   tramp - in', ___   Tryin' to make Heav-en my home,

Call   F   *Response*   C   F   *End (Fine)*

I'm tramp-in', ___   tramp - in', ___   Tryin' to make Heav-en my home.

Verse
Call   F

I've   nev - er been   to Heav - en   but   I've   been   told,

Response
F   C   F   *Call*

Tryin' to make Heav-en my   home,   The streets up there are

F   *Response*   C   *Go back to the beginning and sing to the End*
F   *(Da Capo al Fine)*

paved with gold,   Tryin' to make Heav-en my   home.

Spotlight on Performance

Spotlight on Performance

Broadway For Kids

MTI's BROADWAY junior

SCHOOLHOUSE ROCK LIVE! Jr.

Mini musicals specifically designed for classroom study and presentation, featuring scenes and songs from the musical Schoolhouse Rock Live! Junior.

Originally conceived and directed by Scott Ferguson
Book by Scott Ferguson, Kyle Hall, and George Keating
Music and Lyrics by Lynn Ahrens, Bob Dorough, Dave Frishberg, Kathy Mandry, George Newall, Tom Yohe

Musical Numbers

The Preamble

Three Is a Magic Number

Interplanet Janet

Interjections

Schoolhouse Rock Live! Jr.
Harris County Carver Middle School,
Hamilton, GA

About Rehearsals

You are about to begin rehearsals for a mini production of *Schoolhouse Rock Live! Jr. Rehearsing* means learning and practicing a show. Below are some words actors use during rehearsals.

Upstage
The area onstage farthest away from the audience.

Stage right
The area of the stage to the actor's RIGHT as she or he faces the audience.

Stage left
The area of the stage to the actor's LEFT as she or he faces the audience.

Downstage
The area onstage closest to the audience.

About the Script

CHARACTER NAMES are colored **RED**

DIALOGUE is colored **BLUE**

STAGE DIRECTIONS are colored *GREEN*

Scene 1

CHILD 1: Welcome to the theatre!

CHILD 2: Let's put on a show!

CHILD 3: Which one shall we do?

CHILD 4: Let's see, wait. ... *(Pauses, shrugs.)* I don't know.

CHILD 5: We've got lessons to learn!

CHILD 6: We've got time on the clock!

CHILD 7: We're all right here at school. ...

ALL: Why not do SCHOOLHOUSE ROCK!?

(ALL improvise reactions such as "yeah," "that sounds great," etc., as a large scroll is unrolled that reads "SCHOOLHOUSE ROCK LIVE!".)

CHILD 8: Remember those cartoons that you saw on TV about grammar, life, and the great number three?

CHILD 9: Remember "Interplanet Janet"?

CHILD 10: I LOVED that one!

CHILD 11: And singing along with the show was such fun!

CHILD 12: But where should we start?

CHILD 13: We won't keep you guessin'!

ALL: Let's kick things off with a HISTORY lesson!

(Another scroll with "THE PREAMBLE" is unrolled.)

CHILD 14: Presenting the UNITED STATES CONSTITUTION!

The Preamble

CD 13:23

Words and Music by
Lynn Ahrens

All
Hey, do you know a - bout the U. S. A.?

5 Do you know a - bout the gov - ern - ment? Can you tell me 'bout the

8 Con - sti - tu - tion? Hey,

11 learn a - bout the U. S. A.!

Solo
18 In sev - en - teen eight - y - sev - en, I'm told, our found - ing fa - thers

21 did a - gree to write a list of prin - ci - ples for

All
24 keep - in' peo - ple free. The U. S. A. was

27 just start - ing out, a whole brand new coun - try.

30 And so our peo - ple spelled it out, the things that we should

More

293

Scene 2

CHILD 15: That number was great! I learned a lot.

CHILD 16: Speaking of numbers, what else have we got?

CHILD 17: Which song was your favorite?

CHILD 18: My favorite, let's see ... my favorite number's the one about three!

ALL: Yeah, yeah ... let's do it!, I love that one!, (etc.).

(A scroll, reading "THREE IS A MAGIC NUMBER," is unrolled.)

Schoolhouse Rock Live! is one of theater's most creative shows. It is based on the 1970s cartoon series, *Schoolhouse Rock!* The musical uses different styles of music to teach subjects such as grammar, science, math, and American history.

Schoolhouse Rock Live! Jr., Harris County Carver Middle School, Hamilton, GA

295

Three Is a Magic Number

CD 13:24

Words and Music by
Bob Dorough

All
One, two, three.

Trio 1
Three is a mag-ic num-ber. Yes, it is,

Trio 2
it's a mag-ic num-ber. Some-where in the

veil of an-cient his-to-ry, you get three

Trio 3
as a mag-ic num-ber. The past and the pres-ent and the

Trio 4   *Trio 5*
fu-ture, faith and hope and char-i-ty, the

heart and the brain and the bo-dy give you three as a mag-ic

All
num-ber. A man and a wo-man had

a lit-tle ba-by. Yes, they did.

Scene 3

CHILD 19: Math is great, now, don't get me wrong ...
But what about science?

CHILD 20: I've got JUST the song ...

(A scroll is unrolled, reading "INTERPLANET JANET" across it.)

CD 13:25

Words and Music by
Lynn Ahrens

They say our so-lar sys-tem is cen-tered a-round the sun.___ Nine plan-ets large and small pa-rad-ing by. But___ some-where out in space there's an-oth-er shin-ing face that you might see some night up in the sky wav-ing "Hi!"___

41 Jan - et got an au - to - graph!_ Uh, huh!_

44 Mer - cu - ry was near the sun so Jan - et stopped by,___ but the

46 mer - cu - ry on Mer - cu - ry was much too high,___ so

48 Jan - et split for Ve - nus, but on Ve - nus she found_ she

50 could - n't see a thing for all the clouds a - round._

Duo

52 Earth looked ex - cit - ing, kind of green and in - vit - ing, so

All

54 Jan - et thought she'd give it a go. But the

56 crea - tures on that plan - et looked so ver - y weird to Jan - et, she

All

58 did - n't e - ven dare to say "Hel - lo." It's a bird!_ It's a plane!_

Why, it must be a U. F. O.! But it was

% Refrain

In - ter - plan - et Jan - et, she's a gal - ax - y girl, a

so - lar sys - tem Ms. from a fu - ture world. She

trav - els like a rock - et with her com - et team, and there's

nev - er been a plan - et Jan - et has - n't seen. No, there's

to Coda

nev - er been a plan - et Jan - et has - n't seen.

Solo *Solo*

Mars is red, and Ju - pi - ter's big, and

Solo

Sat - urn shows off its rings. U - ra - nus is built on a

Solo *All*

fun - ny tilt, and Nep - tune is its twin. And

More

D.S. al Coda

82 Plu-to, lit-tle Plu-to, is the far-thest plan-et from our sun.___

Coda

86 has - n't seen.___

Scene 4

(The song ends and the CHILDREN
begin putting their PROPS away.)

CHILD 21: Is there time for one more?

CHILD 22: If we don't dilly-dally!

CHILD 23: Here's my favorite song, for the big grand finale!

ALL: "INTERJECTIONS!" Yea!

(TWO CHILDREN go to CENTER; one coughing and sneezing,
the other playing a doctor.)

Schoolhouse Rock Live! Jr., Gowanda Elementary School, Gowanda, NY

Interjections

CD 13:26

Words and Music by Lynn Ahrens

When Re-gi-nald was home with the flu,_ uh-huh. The doc-tor knew just what_ to do.__ She cured the in-fec - tion with one small in-jec - tion, while Re-gi-nald ut-tered some in - ter - jec - tions.

Solo 1:
Hey! That smarts!

Solo 2:
Ouch! That hurts!

Solo 3:
Yow! That's not fair, givin' a guy a shot down there!

Small Group

(Hey!) (Ouch!) (Yow!)

17 In - ter - jec-tions show ex-cite-ment or e - mo-tion. They're

19 gen-er-al - ly set a - part from a sen-tence by an ex - cla - ma-tion point,

3

21 or by a com - ma when the feel - ing's not as strong. So when you're

Small Group

23 hap - py, (Hur - ray!) or sad, (Aw!) or

25 fright-ened, (Eek!) or mad, (Rats!) or ex -

27 ci - ted, (Wow!) or glad, (Hey!) an

2

29 in - ter - jec - tion starts a sen - tence right!

33 The game was tied at sev - en all,___ uh - huh, when

36 Frank-lin found he had_ the ball._ He made a con-nec - tion in the

39 oth-er di-rec - tion, the crowd start-ed shout-in' out in - ter - jec-tions.

Solo 1:
Aw! You threw
the wrong way!

Solo 2:
Darn! You just
lost the game! **4**

Solo 3:
Hurray! I'm for
the other team!

42

*Small
Group*

(Aw!)   (Darn!)   (H'ray!)

46 In - ter - jec-tions   show ex - cite-ment   or e - mo-tion.   They're

48 gen-er-al - ly set   a - part from a sen - tence   by an ex - cla - ma-tion point,

50 or   by a com - ma when the feel - ing's   not   as   strong.

52 In - ter - jec-tions   show ex - cite-ment   or e - mo-tion.   Hal-le -

Solo 1:
Darn! That's the end!

54 lu - jah.   Hal-le - lu - jah.   Hal-le - lu - jah.___ Yeah!

★ **Take a Bow**

305

At the Movies

Many movies have a special song. Think of a song from your favorite movie. After you saw the movie, what made you remember the song? Here are four great movie songs that you will enjoy singing. You might even know some of them already!

SKILL BUILDER: Eye Contact and Posture

When you are standing on stage at a concert, there are many interesting things to look at. To be a good performer, it is important to keep your eyes on the conductor and stand with good posture.

Follow these steps for good posture when you sing:

• Stand with your feet about shoulder width apart.
• Keep your back straight.
• Place your hands at your sides.

All it takes are the first few notes and the finger snaps. You know right away: It's the creepy tune from *The Addams Family*!

THE ADDAMS FAMILY THEME

from the movie *The Addams Family*

CD 14:1

Words and Music by Vic Mizzy

1. They're
creep-y and they're kook-y,   mys-te-ri-ous and spook-y,   they're
house is a   mu-se-um,   where peo-ple come to   see 'em,   they

al-to-geth-er ook-y,   the Add-ams Fam-i-ly.   2. Their
real-ly are a scree-um,   the Add-ams Fam-i-ly.

Finger snaps

Neat!   Sweet!   Pe-tite!   So

get a witch-'s shawl on,   a broom-stick you can crawl on,   we're

gon-na pay a call on   the Add-ams Fam-i-ly.

The Add-ams Fam-i-ly.

CONCEPT
MELODY
SKILLS
SING

Have you ever been to the circus? There is excitement everywhere you look: scary lions, goofy clowns, flying trapeze artists, and much more. "The Greatest Show on Earth" is a song from a movie that is all about the circus. When you sing this song, you might feel like you are sitting in the audience!

from the movie *The Greatest Show on Earth*

CD 14:4

Music by Victor Young
Words by Ned Washington

1. Come to the cir - cus and laugh your cares a -
   men - dous, stu - pen - dous as cir - cus - es should

way. Come to the cir - cus! See the cir - cus!
be! The Ben - gal ti - ger and the li - on,

If we're not ve - ry care - ful life can o - ver - work us.
the tra - peze art - ist does a leap that's death de - fy - ing.

Come see the clowns who play their part, and wear a
A land of mirth, your mon - ey's

smile though they hide a bro - ken heart._____ 2. Tre -

worth, come on a - long to the cir - cus, the great-est show on

Earth. The hu - man can - non - ball will

zoom, as trum-pets blare and bass drums boom.

Who en - ter-tained your mom and pop? The peo - ple

un - der the great Big Top!

CONCEPT
MELODY
SKILLS
SING

The Muppet Movie tells the story of how the Muppets became famous. In the beginning of the movie, Kermit the Frog sings this song about a rainbow. Rainbows mean different things for different people. What do you think of when you see a rainbow in the sky?

The Rainbow Connection

from *The Muppet Movie*

Words and Music by
Paul Williams and Kenny Ascher

CD 14:7

Moderately, with a lilt

1. Why are there so man-y
2. Who said that ev'-ry wish would
3. Have you been half a-sleep and

songs a-bout rain-bows, And what's on the oth-er
be heard and an-swered, When wished on the morn-ing
have you heard voic-es? I've heard them call-ing my

side?_____ Rain-bows are vi-sions but
star?_____ Some-bo-dy thought of that, and
name._____ Is this the sweet sound that

on-ly il-lu-sions, And rain-bows have noth-ing to
some-one be-lieved it Look what it's done___ so
calls the young sail-ors? The voice might be one and the

CONCEPT
MELODY
SKILLS
SING

Fairy tales have happy endings when the characters believe in themselves and their dreams. In the movie *Shrek*, Shrek doesn't get upset by things other people think about him. His dreams come true because he believes in himself.

I'm a Believer

CD 14:10

from the movie *Shrek*

Words and Music by Neil Diamond

1. I thought love was on-ly true__ in fair-y tales, meant for some-one else but not for me. Love was out to get me. That's the way it seemed.__ Dis-ap-point-ment haunt-ed all my dreams.

2. I thought love was more or less__ a giv-in' thing. Seems the more__ I gave, the less I got. What's the use in try-in'? All you get is pain.__ When I want-ed sun-shine, I got rain.

Then I saw her face. Now I'm__ a be-liev - er.

23 Not a trace of doubt_ in my mind.

27 I'm in love. I'm__ a be-liev - er. I could-n't leave_

1. 31 _____ her if I tried.

2. tried. Then I saw her

Sing 3 times 36 face. Now I'm__ a be-liev - er.

LISTENING CD 14:13

My Favorite Things from *The Sound of Music*

by Richard Rodgers and Oscar Hammerstein II

Listen to Julie Andrews and the children from the movie *The Sound of Music* sing "My Favorite Things." The movie was originally written as a musical for the stage, but most people know this beautiful song from the movie.

Scene from *The Sound of Music*

The Shore Thing

Ahoy there, matey! Visiting the ocean shore can be exciting. You can ride the waves, relax in the sunshine, or take a boat trip to go fishing. You may discover many amazing sea creatures, too. When you sing the next few songs, imagine you are at the shore. Don't forget your swim suit!

VOICE BUILDER: Breathing

Good singers make sure they control their breathing. You can begin to learn to control your breathing with these exercises:

• Imagine you are holding a milkshake as large as the room. Drink the air through a giant straw.

• As you breathe in, imagine that your ribs grow larger.

Practice your breath control by singing this exercise.

ah___ ah___ ah___

CD 14:14

Steadily

American Folk Song

1. When o'er the si-lent seas a-lone, for days and nights we've
sails a-back we near-er come; kind words are said of

8 cheer - less gone, Oh! they who've felt it know how sweet some
friends and home; but soon, too soon we part in pain to

to Coda

11 sun - ny morn_ a sail to meet, some sun - ny morn a sail to meet!
sail the si - lent seas a - gain, to

Refrain

15 Spark - ling on deck is ev' - ry eye: Ship a - hoy! ship a - hoy! our

18 joy - ful cry when an - sw'ring back we faint - ly hear: Ship a -

D.S. al Coda

21 hoy! ship a - hoy! What cheer! what cheer!_____ 2. Now_

⊕ **Coda**

24 sail the si - lent seas a - gain.

CONCEPT
MELODY
SKILLS
SING

This silly song comes from the province of Newfoundland, which is in Canada. A herring is a type of fish that lives in the Atlantic and Pacific Oceans. Many people in Newfoundland like herrings so much, they sing a song about them.

MAP

UNITED STATES   NEWFOUNDLAND

THE HERRING

CD 14:17

Folk Song from Newfoundland, Canada

With gusto

1. O what will we do with the old her-rings' heads? We'll get some loaves and sell them for bread. O
2. O what will we do with the old her-rings' fins? We'll get some nee-dles and sell them for pins. O
3. O what will we do with the old her-rings' backs? We'll get a boy and we'll call him Jack. O
4. O what will we do with the old her-ring's scales? We'll get some can-vas and sew it for sails. O

Repeat second, third, and fourth time singing previous rhymes in reverse order

9
her - rings' heads and loaves_ of bread, and all things like
her - rings' fins and nee-dles for pins,
her - rings' back and boy__ called Jack,
her - rings' scales and can-vas for sails,

12
that. And of all the fish that's in the sea, the her - ring is the

16
fish for me. Right did-dy she loo-ra, right she loo-ra fol-a-dol dee.__

LISTENING   CD 14:20

Two in a Boat American Folk Song

Children who grow up on the shore often sing songs about the water. "Two in a Boat" is a fun song that children sing in different parts of the United States.

Listen to the Revels Children's Chorus perform this song. They pronounce the words very clearly. This helps the audience understand the meaning of the song.

Revels Children's Chorus members sing and dance at Harvard University, Cambridge, Massachusetts.

All over the world, people love the sound of the sea. "El arroyo que murmura" is a folk song from Cuba. It describes the gentle sound of a brook as it winds its way to the sea. How do the melody and rhythm of the song make you feel?

MAP

UNITED STATES

CUBA

El arroyo que murmura

The Murmuring Brook

CD 14:21

Folk Song from Cuba
English Words by Ruth De Cesare

Moderately

Spanish: El a - rro - yo que mur - mu - ra y que la lu - na re -
Pronunciation: el a ɾo yo ke muɾ mu ɾa i ke la lu na ɾe -
English: Mur - mur - ing brook is so love - ly as it's re - flect - ed in

8 tra - ta, cuan-do sus ra - yos de pla - ta a - tra-vie-san la es-pe-
tra ta kwan do sus ɾa yos ðe pla ta a tɾa ßye san les pe
moon-beams. Sil - ver rays cross-ing the dark - ness make it ap-pear as a

12 su - ra. El sin - son - te de voz pu - ra
su ɾa el sin son te ðe ßos pu ɾa
sweet dream. Soon the mock-ing-bird's sing-song will

318

CONCEPT
FORM
SKILLS
SING

Wouldn't it be great to travel underwater in your very own submarine? You could take your friends to explore underwater caverns and chase gigantic octopuses. The famous pop group the Beatles thought this would be neat, too. They wrote about an imaginary trip in the song "Yellow Submarine."

YELLOW SUBMARINE

CD 14:25

Words and Music by
John Lennon and Paul McCartney

1. In the town____ where I was born lived a
   sailed____ up to the sun till we

man____ who sailed the sea, and he told____ us of his
found____ the sea of green, and we lived____ be-neath the

life in the land____ of sub-ma-rines. 2. So we
waves in our yel-low____ sub-ma-rine.

We all live in a Yel-low Sub-ma-rine, Yel-low Sub-ma-rine,

Yel-low Sub-ma-rine. We all live in a Yel-low Sub-ma-rine, Yel-low Sub-ma-rine,

Fine

Yel-low Sub-ma-rine 3. And our friends___ are all a-board; man-y
4. As we live___ a life of ease, ev'-ry-

more of them___ live next door, and the band___ be-gins to
one of us___ has all we need, sky of blue___ and sea of

1.
2.   *D.S. al Fine*

play: green in our yel-low___ sub-ma-rine.

Early in America

Life in the early days of the United States was very different from today. In these early times, many different groups of people helped build our country. Native Americans, African Americans, Europeans, and many other groups all shared parts of their culture.

The Minutemen were a group of American soldiers during the Revolutionary War. They named themselves the Minutemen because they said they could be ready for anything in a minute. Here is a song about these soldiers. Guess how long it takes to sing it!

The Minuteman Minute Song

CD 14:28

Music by Mary Lynn Lightfoot
Words by Lee Brandon

Spirited

Min - ute-man! Min-ute-man! Read - y in on - ly a

min-ute! 1. In the time it takes to sing this song, the Min-ute-man so
   time it takes to sing this song, the Min-ute-man with

brave and strong; put a - side his work or play and came a - run - ning
mus - ket long; took the green at Lex - ing - ton and faced the Red - coats

night or day, in the time it takes to sing this song!   2. In the
in the sun, in the time it takes to sing this

21 song! 3. In the time it takes to sing this song, the

25 Con-cord Min-ute-man so strong; faced the Brit-ish flag un-furled; a

29 shot was heard a-round the world in the time it takes to sing this

grad. accel. to end

33 song! 4. In the time it takes to sing this song, the Min-ute-man so

38 brave and strong; put a-side his work or play and came a-run-ning

f

42 night or day,_____ in the time it takes to sing this song!

VOICE BUILDER: Singing Phrases

To be a good singer, it is important to sing long phrases
well. Practice these steps while you sing the exercise below:

- Imagine your mouth is shaped like a tall tree. Keep the
  corners of your mouth from spreading outward.
- Change smoothly from one note to the next.
- Use good breath control.

ah_____
oh_____

African Americans have played an important part in the history of the United States. "Open the Window, Noah" is an African American **spiritual**. This is one style that African Americans created in the 1800s.

CD 15:1

African American Spiritual

CONCEPT
MELODY
SKILLS
SING

In early American times, Native American people lived all over North America. The "Buffalo Dance Entrance Song" is sung by a group of Native Americans called the Hopi who live in Arizona. This song begins a Hopi ceremony. It welcomes dancers to the center of the village.

Buffalo Dance Entrance Song

CD 15:4

Hopi Social Dance Song
As sung by Tsung-ayeh (Wil Numkena)

ya   ya   he   ha - a   we   yo - o   ha   ya

ya   ya   we   ha - a   we   yo - o   ha   ya   he

ya   he   ha - a   we   ya   e   ya   yo - o _____   we

ya   e   ha - a   we   ya - a   he - e   na

Fourth time end
(Fine)

he - e   yo   ha   he   yo   we   ha ___   hi   ye   ne - e   ya

CONCEPT
MELODY
SKILLS
SING

"In Good Old Colony Times" is a silly American folk song about three troublemakers. They lived in the time before the United States became independent. When you sing this song, you will discover the trouble these three get themselves into.

In Good Old Colony Times

CD 15:8

American Folk Song
Words adapted by Phyllis Kaplan

1. In___ good old col-on-y times when___ we___ lived un-der the king, Three___ rogu-ish chaps fell in-to mis-haps, be-cause they could not sing,

2. O the first he was___ a mil-ler and the sec-ond he was___ a wea-ver, And the third he was a tail-or man, Three rogu-ish chaps to-ge-ther.

3. O the mil-ler, he___ stole corn; and the wea-ver, he___ stole yarn, And the tai-lor man ran right___ a-way with the broad-cloth un-der his arm.

4. The___ mil-ler was drowned in the dam, and the wea-ver got hung___ in his yarn, And the tai-lor tripped as he ran___ a-way with the broad-cloth un-der his arm.

Be-cause they could not sing, Be-cause they could not sing, Three___ rogu-ish chaps fell in-to mis-haps, be-cause they could not sing.

CONCEPT
RHYTHM
SKILLS
SING

Many African Americans settled on islands off the coast of Georgia, called the Georgia Sea Islands. "Uncle Jessie" is a song that children from the Georgia Sea Islands sing.

Uncle Jessie

CD 15:11

Georgia Sea Islands Folk Song

With conviction, Moderato

1. Now, here comes Un - cle Jes - sie. Com-ing through the
2. Now, here comes Un - cle Jes - sie. He's look-ing ve - ry
3. Now, if you want a sweet-heart I'll tell you what to

field, With his horse and bug - gy and I know just how he
sad. He's lost his cot - ton and his corn and ev' - ry-thing he
do, Just take some salt and pep - per and sprin-kle it in your

feels.
had. } Walk, walk, Un-cle Jes-sie, walk, walk, walk. Un-cle Jes-sie
shoe.

walk, walk, Step, Un-cle Jes-sie, step, step, step, Un-cle Jes-sie, step.

 LISTENING CD 15:14

| **Uncle Jessie** African American Folk Song

Listen to Janice Turner sing "Uncle Jessie." She learned this song on the playground when she was young. How would you describe her voice?

Honoring Our World

We share the world with many different people, animals, and plants. If we want our planet to stay healthy, we need to respect all these living things. It is important for us to leave the world healthy for people in the future. Here are some songs that will help us remember to take care of Earth.

SKILL BUILDER: How Did You Do?

When you finish practicing or performing, it is always good to take a minute to think about how you sang a piece. You can think about your own performance. You can also think about your choir's performance. Thinking and talking about your performance helps you find ways you can improve.

Here are some questions you can ask yourself after you sing:
- Was this a good performance? Why or why not?
- How could I sing this song better?
- How could my choir sing this song better?
- What parts of this song are hard for me to sing?
- Did I look at the conductor during the entire song?

CD 15:15

OH MAMA BAKUDALA

Xhosa Folk Song

Xhosa: **Oh   ma-ma ba-ku-da-la ba-be   than - da-za.**
Pronunciation: o   ma ma ba ku da la   ba be   tan   da za

Ba - be   than - da-za,   ba-be   than - da-za.
ba be   tan   da za   ba be   tan   da za

CONCEPT
RHYTHM
SKILLS
SING

"I Walk in Beauty" was written by a Native American woman named Arlene Nofchissey Williams who is from the Navajo tribe. Many Native Americans now perform versions of her song in their own traditional languages. For the Navajo people, beauty means living in harmony with the world.

I WALK IN BEAUTY

CD15:19

Words and Music by
Arlene Nofchissey Williams

Heh neh - yah - nah heh yah heh yah - nah heh neh - yah - nah

heh yah hee yoh___ heh yah hee yoh.   ___ heh yah hee yoh.   I

yearn for Beau - ty,   yes I do, yes I do; I learn of___ Beau - ty,

yes I do, you know I do; I beam with Beau - ty,   just for you and on - ly you, heh

yah,___ heh yah hee yoh.   Heh neh - yah - nah, hey yah heh yah - nah,

Heh neh - yah - nah, heh yah hee yoh_____ Heh yah nee yoh.

CONCEPT
FORM
SKILLS
SING

Raffi is a songwriter from Canada. He has written songs for children for many years. Many of his songs have a message that tells people to take good care of our world. After you learn to sing "Evergreen, Everblue," share its message with your friends and family.

Evergreen, Everblue

CD 15:23

Words and Music by Raffi

Ev-er-green,_ ev - er - blue, As it was in the be-gin-ning,_ we've got to see it through._ Ev-er-green,_ ev - er - blue, At this point in time, it's up to me, it's up to you.

3. So come

1., 2., 3.

4.

Fine

1. Am - a - zon is call-ing,
2. O - cean's wave is rumbling,
(3.) all u - nit - ed na-tions,

Help this plan-et Earth!

With
With

voic - es from the jun - gle,
voic - es from the sea - way,
Chil-dren of one moth - er,

Help this plan-et Earth!

With

30

Hear the tree that's fall - ing,
Wa - ter's for the drink - ing,
love for one a - noth - er,

Help this plan-et Earth!

Be -
For our

D.C. after Verses 1 and 2
D.C. al Fine after Verse 3

34

Rain for - ests___ are cry - ing,
lu - ga whales_ are sing - ing,
sons' and daugh - ters' fu - ture,

Help this plan-et Earth_ to stay:

 LISTENING CD 15:26

Have to Have a Habitat by Bill Oliver

Listen to Bill Oliver sing "Have to Have a Habitat." Habitats are places where people and animals live, like forests, oceans, or fields. Bill is also known as "Mr. Habitat." Everywhere he goes he sings a message to respect the planet.

CONCEPT
RHYTHM
SKILLS
SING

There is one easy way for everyone to help keep our world healthy and clean: Recycle! Glass, newspapers, plastic bottles, and cans are only some of the things we can recycle. "Recycle Rap" will get your head nodding to the beat and make you want to clean up the trash at your feet.

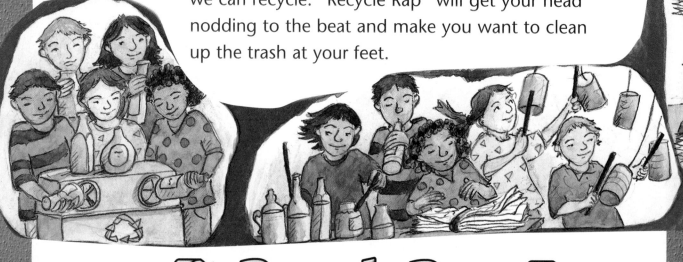

Recycle Rap

CD 15:27

Words and Music by Teresa Jennings

Lis-ten up, friends, you've got to help with our plan. Or we could

all be liv-in' in a gar-bage can. Just save your glass and your tin cans, a-

lu - mi - num, too. Re - cy - cling is the thing to do!

Re - cy - cle, re - cy - cle, re - cy - cle, now! There's noth - in' to it if you

just know how. So tell your bro - ther and your sis - ter and your tea - cher, too:

Club Music

Have you ever wanted to join a club? The four songs in this theme are about a special music club. All the club members love to sing, and everyone is welcome to share their songs. The excitement begins as soon as you open the door to the clubhouse. Sing "Consider Yourself" and join the club!

VOICE BUILDER: Singing Vowels

Vowels are a very important part of singing. When you sing vowels, make your mouth into the shape of an oval. Keep your jaw loose and relaxed, too. Your voice will then mix well with other people's voices.

The five basic vowel sounds are: *oo, oh, ee, eh, ah.* Use these sounds to sing the exercise below:

Repeat at higher pitch levels

oo_____   oo_____   oo_____
oh_____   oh_____   oh_____
ee_____   ee_____   ee_____
eh_____   eh_____   eh_____
ah_____   ah_____   ah_____

 LISTENING CD 15:30

Consider Yourself from *Oliver!* by Lionel Bart

Listen to the cast from the movie *Oliver!* sing "Consider Yourself." The characters in *Oliver!* are from London, England. Do they sing the words differently than you? How are they different?

Consider Yourself

CD 16:1   from the musical *Oliver!*

Words and Music by Lionel Bart

1. Con - sid - er your-self ___ at home,   Con-sid-er your-self ___
sid-er your-self ___ well in: Con-sid-er your-self ___

___ one of the fam - i - ly   We've tak-en to you ___ so strong.
___ part of the fur - ni - ture.   There is - n't a lot ___ to spare;

It's clear   we're   go-ing to get a-long! 2.Con-
Who cares?   What -   ev - er we've got we share!

Con - sid - er your-self ___ our mate,   We don't want to have ___

___ no fuss   For   af - ter some con - sid - er - a - tion,

1.
we can   state: Con - sid-er your-self ___ one of us.   2. Con -

2.
sid-er your - self ___   one of us. ___

CONCEPT
MELODY

SKILLS
SING

The music club sings many different music styles. They sing along with pop songs on the radio and the golden oldies, too. But one style they all love is dance songs. You will feel the swinging beat as you sing this song. It will make you want to "Flip, Flop and Fly!"

Flip, Flop and Fly

CD 16:4

from the movie *Chicken Run*

Words and Music by
Charles E. Calhoun and Lou Willie Turner

When I get the blues gon-na get me a rock-in' chair. When I get the blues gon-na get me a rock-in' chair. When the blues o-ver-take me, gon-na rock right a-way from here.

Flip, flop, fly,__ I'll see you by and by.__

CONCEPT
HARMONY
SKILLS
SING

One day the kids arrive at the clubhouse and something has eaten all the snacks. They discover big paw prints on the ground outside the door. It looks like a bear has broken in! Where did the bear go? Sing this song and imagine you have joined their search.

Look High, Look Low

CD 16:7

Words and Music by
John Jacobson and John Higgins

Determined march style

mf

Look high! Look low! Look ev'-ry-where that a

8 bear might go. Look in the trees, and look on the ground.

11 Look all a-round and a-round and a-round. Look high! Look low!

15 Look ev' - ry-where that a bear might go. Look o - ver there, look

18 to and fro. Where in the world did she go?

Part I (spoken)
Look un-der there! Up in the air? Here?

Part II (spoken)
21 No bear! No bear! No!

f
There? Where in the world did she go? Look high! Look low!

26 No! Where in the world did she go?

Look ev' - ry-where that a bear might go. Look in the trees, and

31 Look high! Look low! Look ev' - ry-where that a

look on the ground. Look all a - round and a - round and a - round.

34 bear might go. Look in the trees, and look on the ground.

More

Look high! Look low! Look ev'-ry-where that a

37 Look all a-round and a-round and a-round. Look high!

bear might go. Look o-ver there, look to and fro.

40 Look low! Look ev'-ry-where that a bear might go.

ff

Where in the world did she go? Where in the world did she go?

43 Look o-ver there, look to and fro. Where in the world did she go?

CONCEPT
HARMONY
SKILLS
SING

Every year, the kids in the club take a field trip. Some of the club members want to visit the big city and see tall skyscrapers. Other members think the club should go hiking in the mountains. There is only one way to settle this argument: Sing!

with "I Love the Mountains"

CD 16:10

1st time: sing Song #1
2nd time: sing Song #2
3rd time: sing both melodies together

Words and Music by
John Jacobson
and Alan Billingsley

Boom - de-ah - da, boom-de-ah - da, boom-de-ah - da, boom-de-ah - da,

Honk, honk, toot, toot, honk, honk, VROOM! I love the

1.

boom - de-ah - da, boom-de-ah - da, boom-da-ah - da, boom! I love the

Honk, honk, toot, toot,

2.

3.

boom - de-ah - da, boom-de-ah - da,

honk, honk, VROOM! I love the honk, honk, VROOM!

Boom, wo wo wo yeah!

Honk, wo wo wo yeah!

CONCEPT
RHYTHM
SKILLS
PLAY

There Was An Old Lady

—Dennis Lee

There was an old lady
    Whose kitchen was bare,
So she woke up the cat
    Saying, "Time for some air!"

She sent him to buy her
    A can of sardines.
But the cat ambled back
    With a bagful of beans.

She sent him to buy her
    A packet of cheese
But the cat reappeared
    With a carton of bees.

She sent him to buy her
    A brisket of beef.
But the cat hurried home
    With a red autumn leaf.

She sent him to buy her
    A dish of ice cream.
But the cat skated in
    With a whole hockey team.

She sent him to buy her
    A plate of spaghetti.
But the cat strutted up
    With a bride and confetti.

She sent him to buy her
    A thermos of tea.
But the cat waddled back
    With a dinosaur's knee.

The fridge was soon bulging,
    And so was the shelf.
So she phoned for a hot dog
    And fetched it herself.

Voice

Da   da   dum,   da   da dum,   da   da   dum   dum   dum!

CONCEPT
RHYTHM
SKILLS
PLAY

The Gebeta Board

This folk tale comes from Ethiopia, a country in Africa. Learn these music patterns before you read the story.

Play them when you see their symbol in the story.

Once there was a small boy who tended his family's cattle. He would watch them all day grazing on the land. He had nothing to do but count them over and over again.

One day his father carved a beautiful gebeta game board for him from the hard, smooth wood of an olive tree. The boy hugged the game in his arms. He now would have games to play while he tended the cattle.

The next day the boy proudly carried the gebeta board with him to the grazing land. He saw four poor men trying to make a fire to cook their food.

"Come, boy," they called to him. "We are hungry and must cook this meat. Where can we find wood?"

"Take this game board to cook your meal. It will be all the wood you need," said the boy. He handed them the game and sadly walked away.

"Wait! Take this shovel in exchange for your kindness," said the four men. The boy took the shovel and continued to follow the cattle.

He soon saw a man digging a well with his hands.

"Oh, I shall never find water. And my family is so thirsty," cried the man.

"Here, take my shovel," said the boy. "It will help you reach water quickly."

"Wait! Please take this bag of grain in exchange," called the man. The boy thanked him, took the bag of grain, and continued on. After a while he saw a mother and her hungry child.

"Oh, where shall we find food. My child is starving," cried the woman.

"Take my bag of grain. It shall keep your family fed for many days," said the boy.

As he walked away the woman cried to him, "We have nothing to give you but this stick of wood. Please take it."

The boy thanked her and began to lead the cattle back home. When he reached the village an old woman cried, "Please may I have your stick of wood? My old husband feels so cold. I must start a fire for him!"

"Of, course," said the boy. He handed her the wood and began to head home.

"Wait!" said the old woman. "Our eyes have grown bad and we can no longer play games. Take our gebeta board in exchange for your kindness." The boy thanked her, led the cattle home and walked in his front door with the board.

"Anything exciting happen today, son?" asked the father.

"Nothing special," said the boy. He sat down with his father on the floor for a long night of games on his gebeta board.

CONCEPT
RHYTHM
SKILLS
PLAY, SING

Isabela and the Troll

This wonderful folk tale comes from Spain. Learn these music patterns before you read the story.

Play them when you see their symbol in the story.

Once upon a time in Spain, there lived an nine-year-old girl with a lovely voice named Isabela.

She lived in a village of white houses. Her favorite thing in the whole world was a coral ring her mother had given her.

One morning Isabela went to the fountain very early. As she walked, she sang her favorite song. When she got there, she took off her coral ring and placed it on the ground. Suddenly, she heard terrible laughter behind her. *Ha, ha, ha!*

Ha, ha, ha!

She turned around to see what it was. Standing behind her was an ugly, gray troll. He was grinning horribly at her. She screamed and tried to run, but he threw a brown sack over her and tossed her over his shoulder. Then he picked up the ring and put it in his pocket.

"My fortune is now made!" giggled the troll. The troll took his sack to the main plaza in the village.

"Here I have a singing sack. Magic's in it, too. Place some money in my hat and it will sing for you." Many people gathered and tossed coins in the hat.

The troll shook the sack and whispered to the girl, "Sing, sing, sing or I'll keep your little ring." Isabela was afraid, so she began to sing. The people were amazed and threw more coins into the hat.

That night he carried the sack to a house in the village and knocked on the door. Isabela's mother answered. The troll yelled, "Here I have a singing sack. Magic's in it, too. Place some money in my hat and it will sing for you."

Isabela's mother missed her daughter. She placed some coins in the hat to cheer herself up. Isabela began to sing her song, more sadly than before.

"That is my Isabela's voice," thought her mother. "If I call out he will run away. I must think of something."

At the end of the song, Isabela's mother invited the troll in for dinner. After a huge meal, the troll lay his head down on the kitchen table and fell fast asleep.

(Snoring sounds)

Isabela's mother quickly untied the sack and Isabela jumped out into her mother's arms. They grabbed their meanest goat and shoved him into the sack. Then Isabela carefully searched the troll's pockets until she found her coral ring.

In the morning, the troll headed to the next house. When he got there, he whispered, "Sing, sing, sing or I'll keep your little ring," but nothing happened. He pinched the sack but all he heard was "maaaa."

"I'll teach you!" the troll screamed at the sack. He tore it open and to his surprise an angry goat jumped out! The goat was so mad he chased the troll out of the village and far away. And the ugly troll was never seen again!

Spotlight on
Celebrations

Spotlight on Celebrations

Spotlight on Celebrations

PATRIOTIC

CONCEPT
MELODY
SKILLS
SING

Songs for Our Country

Singing songs about pride in our country brings Americans together. Katharine Lee Bates wrote "America, the Beautiful" after a trip to Pike's Peak in Colorado.

America, the Beautiful

CD 16:13

Music by Samuel Ward
Words by Katharine Lee Bates

1. O beau-ti-ful for spa-cious skies, For am-ber waves of grain.
2. O beau-ti-ful for he-roes proved In lib-er-at-ing strife,
3. O beau-ti-ful for pa-triot dream That sees be-yond the years,

For pur-ple moun-tain maj-es-ties A-bove the fruit-ed plain.
Who more than self their coun-try loved, And mer-cy more than life.
Thine al-a-bas-ter cit-ies gleam, Un-dim'd by hu-man tears.

A - mer - i - ca! A - mer - i - ca! God shed His grace on thee,

And crown thy good with broth-er-hood, From sea to shin-ing sea.

You're a Grand Old Flag

Words and Music by George M. Cohan

CD 16:16

You're a grand old flag, you're a high-fly-ing flag;

And for-ev-er in peace may you wave;

You're the em-blem of the land I love,

The home of the free and the brave.

Ev'-ry heart beats true un-der red, white, and blue,

Where there's nev-er a boast or brag;

But should auld ac-quaint-ance be for-got,

Keep your eye on the grand old flag.

Americans like to sing about their country, their people, and their flag.

☆This Is America☆

CD 16:19

Words and Music by Teresa Jennings

This is A - mer - i - ca. A - mer - i - ca.

This is A - mer - i - ca. A - mer - i - ca.

A land of cour - age, faith, and hon - or.

A land of true e - qual - i - ty.

A land of hope and pride. A — land of u - ni - ty.

(2nd time) D.S. al Fine

Fine

A — land of lib - er - ty.

Yankee Doodle Boy

CD 16:22

Words and Music by George M. Cohan

I'm a Yan - kee Doo - dle Dan - dy,

A Yan - kee Doo - dle, do or die;___

A real live neph - ew of my Un - cle Sam,

Born on the Fourth of Ju - ly.___

I've got a Yan - kee Doo - dle sweet - heart,

She's my Yan - kee Doo - dle joy.___

Yan-kee Doo-dle came to Lon-don, just to ride the po - nies,

I am a Yan - kee Doo - dle boy.___

AUTUMN

CONCEPT
METER
SKILLS
SING, LISTEN

Hispanic Heritage Month

September 15 to October 15 is Hispanic Heritage Month in the United States. During this time people celebrate the ways Hispanics have worked to help make our country great. People from many backgrounds gather to have fun and learn about Hispanic art, food, culture, and music.

"Pajarillo barranqueño," a song from Mexico, is a favorite at Mexican get-togethers!

Pajarillo barranqueño

Little Bird

CD 16:25

MAP

UNITED STATES → MEXICO

Mexican Folk Song
English Words by Linda Worsley

Spanish: 1. Pa - ja - ri - llo, pa - ja - ri - llo, _____ pa - ja -
Pronunciation: pa xa ɾi yo pa xa ɾi yo pa xa
English: 1. Lit - tle bird, _____ pa - ja - ri - llo, _____ Lit - tle
2. Who is this _____ pa - ja - ri - llo, _____ in the

ri - llo ba - rran - que - ño, _____ ¡qué bo - ni - tos o - jos
ɾi yo βa ɾan ke nyo ke βo ni tos o xos
bird _____ there on the hill - side, _____ Oh, what pret - ty eyes you
tree _____ there sweet - ly sing - ing? _____ Go and tell her not to

tie - nes lás - ti - ma que ten - gan due - ño! _____
tye nes las ti ma ke ten gan dwe nyo
have, and what a shame you have a mas - ter.
sing, be - cause her song has left me weep - ing. _____

LISTENING CD 16:29

Flor de huevo by Los Lobos

The members of Los Lobos have performed together since they were high school friends in Los Angeles, California. They have mixed traditional Mexican music with other styles to come up with their own sound. One member of Los Lobos says that they "like bringing music together to bring people together."

Los Lobos live in Los Angeles, California.

Listen to the first composition of Los Lobos.

Children in Mexico like to say this rhyme to learn to count. Some of the words don't mean anything at all. They are just fun to say!

**Una de dola,
de tela canela,
zumabaca la vaca,
de bire birón.
cuéntalas bien
que las once son:
uno, dos, tres, cuatro,
cinco, seis, siete, ocho,
nueve diez, once.**

CONCEPT
FORM
SKILLS
SING

Sukkot is a harvest festival that lasts for seven days. Jewish people build a small shelter called a *sukkah* and decorate it with autumn fruits and vegetables.

CHAG ASIF
Harvest Time

CD 17:1

Words and Music by S. Levy Tannai
English Version by L. Koulish

Refrain

Hebrew: חַג אָ - סִיף, חַג אָ - סִיף כֵּן יִר - בֶּה דְּ וְ - כֵן יוֹ סִיף.
Pronunciation: xag a sif xag a sif ken yir be və xen yo sif
English: **Har-vest time, har-vest time. Gath-er in the gold-en wheat.**

Verse

ba sa de xa laf ka tsir

1. In the mead - ow as we___ walk,
2. Draw the wa - ter from the___ well,
3. Thanks for days that come and___ go, The

u va ke rem tam ba tsir

Wheat is rip-en - ing on the___ stalk.
See the fruits of har - vest___ swell.
warmth of the sun and the fall - ing___ snow.

360

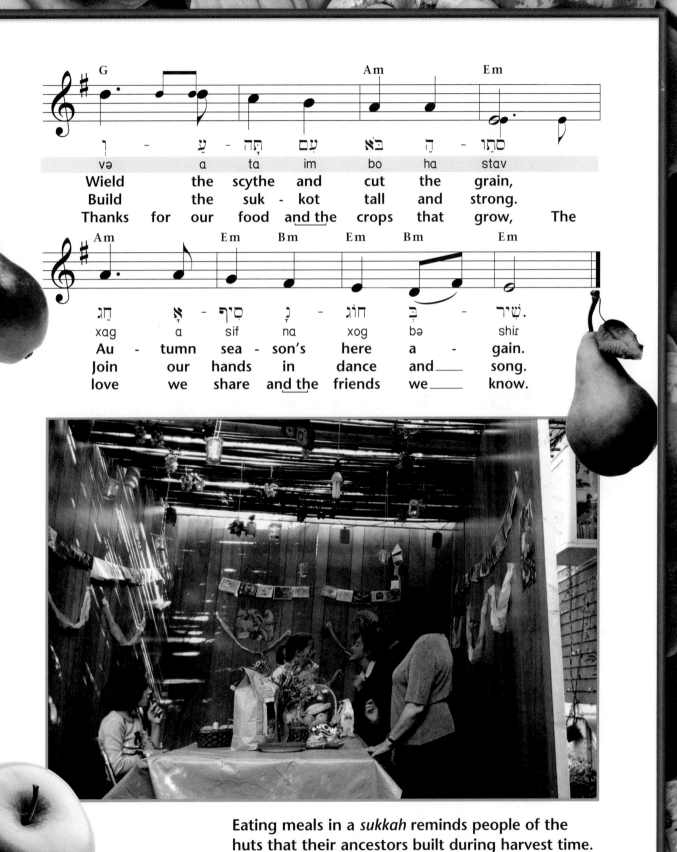

Wield   the   scythe   and   cut   the   grain,
Build   the   suk - kot   tall   and   strong.
Thanks   for   our   food   and the   crops   that   grow,   The

və   a   ta   im   bo   ha   stav

xag   a   sif   na   xog   bə   shir

Au - tumn   sea - son's   here   a - gain.
Join   our   hands   in   dance   and___ song.
love   we   share   and the   friends   we___ know.

Eating meals in a *sukkah* reminds people of the
huts that their ancestors built during harvest time.

CONCEPT
RHYTHM
SKILLS
SING, LISTEN

Will you be meeting some spooky friends on Halloween night? Watch out, or one of them just might say BOO!

CD 17:5

Words and Music by Cheryl Lavender

Danse Macabre (excerpt) by Camille Saint-Saëns

The French composer Camille Saint-Saëns began his musical career when he was a child. By the time he was 22, he was a famous composer. "Danse Macabre" is one of his most popular pieces.

Listening Map for Danse Macabre (excerpt)

Use *Orchestral Instruments* **CD-ROM** to learn more about the violin.

Thanksgiving is a time to be with family and friends. Here is a song about one friend that no Thanksgiving should be without!

CD 17:9

Words and Music by
John Jacobson and Alan Billingsley

1. I have a friend whose name is Tom.
2. Old Tom was lost one au-tumn day.
3. When I sat down to read Tom's will;

Gob-ble gob-ble gig-gle gig-gle did-i-ly bom bom!

Nev-er real-ly knew where he was from.
He just up and wobbled a-way.
Here came Tom wobbling over the hill.

Gob-ble gob-ble gig-gle gig-gle did-i-ly bom bom!

My friend Tom likes to gob-ble when he wob-bles.

My friend Tom likes to wan-der to and fro.

My friend Tom likes to gig-gle when he wig-gles.

My friend Tom is a tur-key don't you know?

My friend Tom is a tur-key don't you know?

Find rhyming words in "My Friend Tom" for 'gobble' and 'giggle.'

Seasonal Songs

Everyone loves this song about a jolly man made of snow.

CD 17:12

Words and Music by
Steve Nelson and Jack Rollins

1. Fros - ty, the Snow-man, was a jol - ly, hap - py soul,_ With a
Fros - ty, the Snow-man, is a fair - y tale, they say,_ He was
Fros - ty, the Snow-man, was a - live as he could be,_ And the

corn - cob pipe and a but - ton nose_ And two eyes made out of coal.
made of snow, but the chil - dren know_ How he
chil - dren say he could laugh and play_ Just the

came to life one day. There
same as you and me.

Coda

must have been some mag-ic in that old silk hat they found; For

(Go back to the beginning then to the 3rd ending.)

when they placed it on his head, He be-gan to dance a-round. Oh,

2. Frosty, the Snowman, knew the sun was hot that day,
So he said, "Let's run and we'll have some fun
Now before I melt away."
Down to the village, with a broomstick in his hand,
Running here and there all around the square,
Sayin' "Catch me if you can."

He led them down the streets of town right to the traffic cop,
And he only paused a moment when he heard him holler "Stop!"
For Frosty, the Snowman, had to hurry on his way,
But he waved good-bye sayin', "Don't you cry,
I'll be back again some day."

CONCEPT
TONALITY
SKILLS
SING

The story of Hanukkah tells of how a little oil kept the holy lamps in a temple in Jerusalem burning for eight days. The holiday is celebrated by lighting candles. Families gather each evening to watch the candles being lit.

Oy Chanuke

CD 17:15

Yiddish Words by M. Rivesman
Jewish Folk Song
English Words by MMH

Yiddish:	אוי	ח	נו-כה	,אוי-ח	נו-כה,	אַ	טוב-יון	אַ	שיי-נער,	אַ		
Pronunciation:	o	xɑ	nu kɑ	o xɑn	u kɑ	ɑ	yɔn tɛf	ɑ	she nər	ɑ		
English:	O	Ha-nuk-kah,		O	Ha-nuk-kah,	a	beau-ti-ful		sea-son,	a		

Yiddish:	לוס-טי-קער,	אַ	פריי-לע-כער,	ני	-טאָ	נאָך	אַ	זוי -נער.		
Pronunciation:	lus tig ər	a	fre lix ər	ni	to	nox	a	zoi nər		
English:	joy-ous	hap-py	fes-ti-val	un-like		an-y		oth-er.		

368

Spin - ning, turn - ing drey - dls and good things to eat;

Hot and tast - y lat - kes are there for a treat.

Come, chil - dren, come, hur - ry; light Ha - nuk - kah can - dles to - night.

Now, ev' - ry - one sing of the won - ders of old, then come

1. join in a cir - cle and dance. Now,

2. join in a cir - cle and dance.

CONCEPT
FORM
SKILLS
SING

The Eight Days of Hanukkah!

CD 17:19

Words and Music by George David Weiss

Verse

Solo Dm — A7 — Group A7
"One" is for the tem-ple walls that did-n't fall. (Did-n't fall.)

Solo Dm — A7 — Group
"Two" is for the men who fought, God bless 'em all. (Bless 'em all.)

Solo Gm — Gm — Dm
"Three" is for the oil they found, e-nough for just one day.

E — E — A7 Bb7 A7 Group
"Four" is for the mir-a-cle that came their way. It burned for eight days.

Solo Dm — A7 — Group A7
"Five" is for the hope and faith that would-n't die. (Would-n't die.)

Solo Dm — Gm — Group
"Six" is for the To-rah scrolls that still sur-vive. (Still sur-vive.)

CONCEPT
RHYTHM
SKILLS
SING

There are presents to buy, boxes to wrap, and yummy goodies to bake. There is so much to do before Christmas day! Sing this song and find out which jolly fellow also has lots to do before the big day!

It's Time to Get Ready for Christmas

CD 17:22

Words and Music by
Emily Crocker and John Higgins

Refrain

It's time to get read-y for Christ-mas.

San-ta's in a hur-ry to pack his sleigh. Time to get read-y for

Christ-mas, soon it will be Christ-mas Day,

soon it will be Christ - mas Day.

Solo 1 *Solo 2*

1. I sew the ears on ted - dy bears. I
2. I il - lus - trate the pic - ture books. I

glue the arms on rock-ing chairs. I paint the let-ters on
tie the strings on fish-ing hooks. I pack up all___ the

build-ing blocks. I wind up all the cuck-oo clocks!
cow-boy hats. I try out all the base-ball bats.

I pump up all the bas-ket-balls. I pin the dia-pers on
I paint the wag-ons shin-y red. I bake up lots of

ba-by dolls. And when their jobs are near-ly done, I
gin-ger-bread. I su-per-vise the toy-shop crew, so

Go back to the beginning, then to Coda
(Da Capo al Coda)

check their work, yes ev-ery-one!
back to work now all of you!

Coda

Soon it will be Christ-mas, soon it will be Christ-mas.

Soon it will be Christ-mas Day!___

CONCEPT
RHYTHM
SKILLS
SING

Get ready to spread some holiday cheer! This popular Christmas song from Wales will put everyone in the holiday spirit!

MAP

UNITED STATES

WALES

CD 17:25

Welsh Carol

1. Deck the hall with boughs of hol - ly, } Fa la la la la, la   la la la,
2. See the blaz - ing   yule be - fore us,
3. Fast a - way the   old year pass - es,

'Tis the sea - son   to   be jol - ly, } Fa la la la la, la   la la la,
Strike the harp and   join the cho - rus,
Hail the new, ye   lads and lass - es,

Don we now our   gay ap - par - el, } Fa la la la la la,   la la la,
Fol - low me in   mer - ry mea - sure,
Sing we joy - ous   all to - geth - er,

Troll the an - cient yule - tide car - ol, } Fa la la la la, la   la la la.
While I tell of yule - tide trea - sure,
Heed - less of the wind and weath - er,

This Christmas carol was first sung many years ago in France.

Listen for which instruments play in "Pat-a-Pan."

CD 17:28

French Carol Tune
English Version by Merrill Staton

1. Wil - lie take your lit - tle drum, Rob-in bring your flute and come.
2. When the lit - tle child was born long a - go that Christ - mas morn,
3. Now we cel - e - brate this day on our in - stru - ments we play.

Play a joy - ous tune to - day.
Shep-herds came from fields a - far, { Tu - re - lu - re - lu, pat-a-pat-a-pan,
Let our voi - ces loud - ly ring,

Play a joy - ous tune to - day on this joy - ous hol - i - day.
Shep-herds came from fields a - far guid - ed by the shin - ing star.
Let our voi - ces loud - ly ring, as our song and gifts we bring.

CONCEPT
TEXTURE
SKILLS
SING, PLAY

CD 18:1

African American Spiritual

Swing *mf*

A - men, A - men,

A - men, A - men, A - men, men. See the (1.) ba - by,
(2.) Moth - er,
(3.) Shep - herds,

Ly - ing in the man - ger,
Sing - in' to the ba - by,
Come to see the ba - by,

One Christ-mas morn - ing,

All

A - men, A-men, A - men.
A - men, A-men, A - men.
A - men, A-men, A -

Go back to the beginning

Solo *p*

men. Sing it soft-er now,

p first time only

All

A - men, A - men,

ff last time only

Solo *f*

A - men, A - men, A - men, Sing it strong-er now, men.

Play this accompaniment as the group sings "Amen."

This African American spiritual is another holiday favorite.

CD 18:4

African American Spiritual

CONCEPT
RHYTHM
SKILLS
SING

When the short parade of the Christmas *posadas* is over, the party begins. Food and drinks like sweet bread and hot chocolate are served. Children may also break a *piñata*!

¡Dale, dale, dale!

CD 18:7

Mexican Folk Song
English Version by MMH

Verse

Spanish: En las no - ches de po - sa - das,
Pronunciation: en las no ches de po sa ðas
English: On the nights of Las Po - sa - das,

la pi - ña - ta_es lo me - jor,
la pi nya ta_es lo me xor
chil - dren strike the bright pi - ña - ta.

Y los ni - ños más a - le - gres
i los ni nyos mas a le gres
See the hap - py, hap - py chil - dren

le pe - gan con gran fer - vor.
le pe gang kong gran fer ßor
as they swing and swing all night.

378

Refrain

C · F · G7 · C

Da - le, da - le, da - le, no pier - das el ti - no,
ða le ða le ða le no pyer ðas el ti no
Da - le, da - le, da - le, do not lose your bal - ance.

C · F · G7 · C

Mi - de la dis - tan - cia, que hay en el ca - mi - no.
mi ðe la ðis tan syn keal en el ka mi no
Turn and turn and turn and you will find your tar - get.

C · F · G7 · C

Que si no le das de un pa - lo te pi - llo,
ke si no le ðas ðeun pa lo te pi yo
For if you should miss it with a cra - zy wild swing,

C · F · G7 · C

Por - que tie - nes ca - ra, de pu - ro zo - rri - llo.___
poɾ ke tye nes ka ɾa ðe pu ɾo so ɾi yo___
You will feel so fool - ish that__ you'll run and hide.__

379

CONCEPT
RHYTHM
SKILLS
SING, LISTEN

Kwanzaa is an African American celebration of the family, community, and culture. It uses words from Swahili, an African language. Kwanzaa lasts seven days. One day celebrates *Ujamaa*. Its message is that people are stronger when everyone works together to help each other.

CD 18:11

Words and Music by Stan Spottswood

1. U - ja - maa means we should cre - ate our own
2. Don't on - ly buy, start to pro - duce. In the

stores and shops and bus-'ness - es.
end, my friend, you'll

have suc - cess.

380

Kuumba is another principle of Kwanzaa. Its message is that when people in a community are creative, the community stays strong. Art and music are ways to express feelings, ideas, and thoughts.

Use *World Instruments* **CD-ROM** to learn more about African instruments.

LISTENING CD 18:14

Chants du Burgam by Doudou N'Diaye Rose

Doudou N'Diaye Rose is from Senegal. He is one of the most famous African drummers in the world.

Art Gallery

Beaded Hair

Music is an important part of what makes a group of people who they are. This painting was created by Amos Ferguson (born in 1920). He was born in the Bahamas. He worked with his father on their farm until he decided to be a painter.

CONCEPT
RHYTHM
SKILLS
LISTEN, SING

Dr. Martin Luther King, Jr., believed that all people should have the same chance in life. He taught that differences in people should bring them together, not separate them.

LISTENING CD 18:15

Down by the Riverside African American Spiritual

People sing songs like this African American spiritual to remember the spirit of Dr. King's message of peace and freedom.

This spiritual tells about the journey to freedom.

I'm on My Way

CD 18:16

African American Spiritual

1. I'm on my way _____ to the free-dom
2. I'll ask my bro-ther _____ to come an go with
3. I'll ask my sis-ter (I'll ask my sis-ter) to come and go with
4. I'm on my way, (I'm on my way) and I won't turn
5. I'm on my way (I'm on my way) to the free-dom

land. _____ I'm on my way _____
me, _____ I'll ask my bro-ther _____
me, (to come and go with me) I'll ask my sis-ter (I'll ask my
back, (and I won't turn back) I'm on my way, (I'm on my
land. (to the free-dom land) I'm on my way, (I'm on my

"Integration is an opportunity to participate in the beauty of diversity."

— Dr. Martin Luther King, Jr.

___	to	the	free - dom	land. ___		
___	to	come and	go with	me, ___		
sis-ter)	to	come and	go with	me,	(to come and	go with
way)	and	I	won't turn	back,	(and I	won't turn
way)	to	the	free - dom	land.	(to the	free - dom

___	I'm	on	my	way ___	to the	free - dom
___	I'll	ask	my	bro-ther ___	to come and	go with
me)	I'll	ask	my	sis-ter (I'll ask my sis-ter)	to come and	go with
back)	I'm	on	my	way, (I'm on my way)	and I	won't turn
land)	I'm	on	my	way (I'm on my way)	to the	free - dom

land, ___			
me, ___			
me, (To come and go with me)	I'm on	my way,	Great
back, (and I won't turn back)			
land, (to the free - dom land)			

God, I'm on my way. ___

383

CONCEPT
MELODY
SKILLS
SING, LISTEN

The Chinese New Year is a time to be with family and friends. It is a time to give thanks. Family members, living and dead, are remembered during this family celebration.

MAP

UNITED STATES — CHINA

Chinese New Year Song

CD 18:19

Traditional Chinese Song
Arranged by Chooi-Theng Lew
English Version by John Higgins

Mandarin: 每 條 大 街 小 巷 每 個 人 的 嘴 裏
Pronunciation: mei tiao da ji shiao shiang mei gʌ ɾʌn di tsuei li
English: **Up and down the streets to-day, There's a joy-ful sound you'll hear.**

見 面 第 一 句 話 都 是 恭 禧 恭 禧
jiɛn miɛn di i chü hwa do shɪ gung shi gung shi
Fam - i - ly and friends all say: Bless-ings for the New Year!

恭 禧 恭 禧 恭 禧 你 呀 恭 禧 恭 禧 恭 禧 你
gung shi gung shi gung shi ni ya gung shi gung shi gung shi ni
Hap-py, hap-py, hap-py New Year! Gong xi, gong xi, gong xi ni!

Use *World Instruments* **CD-ROM** to learn more about Asian instruments.

The Year-Naming Race Chinese Folk Tale

Each year of the Chinese calendar is named for an animal. Listen to a story that tells how the years got their names.

Name the animals of the Chinese calendar.

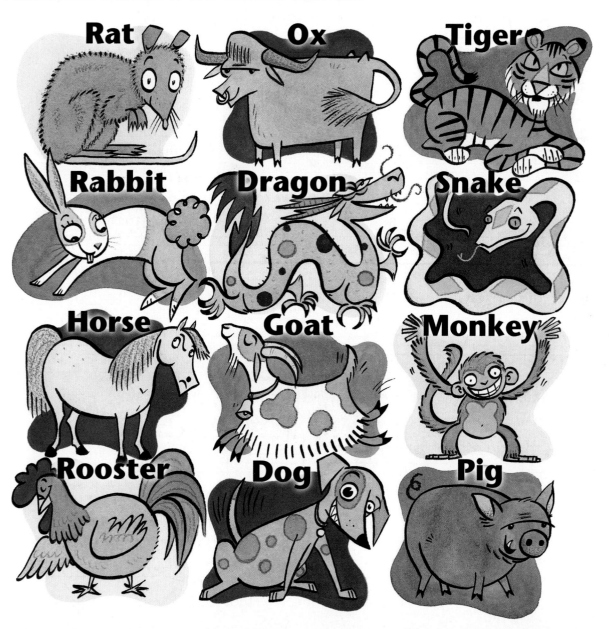

Rat   Ox   Tiger

Rabbit   Dragon   Snake

Horse   Goat   Monkey

Rooster   Dog   Pig

Valentine's Day is a day to remember the ones you love. Show your friends you care. Sing this song with a special friend!

This a Way and That a Way

CD 18:24

Words and Music by
John Jacobson and Alan Billingsley

Refrain

This a way and that a way and that a way and this a way. All that I have to say is, "I like you!" A one way or an - o - ther way, an - oth-er way or a one__ way. All I'm a - bout to say is, "I hope you like me too."__

Verse

When we are sing - ing to - geth - er, we have a beau - ti - ful tone._____ I hope we'll stay friends for - ev - er, 'cause

Go back to the beginning and sing to the End.
(Da Capo al Fine)

I don't like sing - ing a - lone! Oh!

LISTENING CD 18:27

Born to Be with You

Bluegrass Song

Good friends are lucky to find each other. This song was popular in the 1950s. Here it is again in bluegrass style.

CONCEPT
RHYTHM
SKILLS
SING

Abraham Lincoln was born in 1809 in Kentucky, but spent much of his life in Illinois. Because of his courage and strength, he is now known as one of the greatest American presidents.

Out from the Wilderness

CD 18:28

Music Attributed to J. Warner
Words by Robert Quackenbush

1. Ol' Abe Lin-coln came— out from the wil-der-ness,
2. Ol' Abe Lin-coln al-ways spoke for our li-ber-ty,
3. Ol' Abe Lin-coln be - lieved in our free-dom rights, be-

Out from the wil-der - ness, out from the wil-der - ness,
Spoke for our li-ber - ty, spoke for our li-ber - ty,
lieved in our free-dom rights, be-lieved in our free-dom rights,

Ol' Abe Lin-coln came— out from the wil-der ness,
Ol' Abe Lin-coln al-ways spoke for our li-ber - ty,
Ol' Abe Lin-coln be - lieved in our free-dom rights,

Down in Il - li - nois.
Down in Il - li - nois.
Down in Il - li - nois.

Lincoln

Lincoln
stares
from our classroom wall.
History says
he was lanky tall.

History says
that he borrowed books
and some people laughed
at his rumpled looks.

Born in a cabin,
he would be
the President
who set slaves free.

He gave the Gettysburg Address.
Except for George Washington
Lincoln was best
of all presidents,
and wise.

I can sort of see that
when I stare at his eyes.

—*Myra Cohn Livingston*

Abraham Lincoln,
the 16th President
of the United States,
guided the country
through difficult times.

Sing this song about a funny stew.

Mrs. Murphy's Chowder

CD 18:31

Words and Music by Oscar Brand

Won't you bring back, won't you bring back

Mis - sus Mur - phy's chow - der? It was tune - ful, ev - 'ry

spoon - ful made you yo - del loud - er. Af - ter din - ner,

Un - cle Ben used to fill his foun - tain pen

From a plate of Mis - sus Mur - phy's chow - der.

Refrain
faster

It had ice cream, cold cream, ben-zine, gas-o-line,
Sponge cake, beef-steak, mis-take, stom-ach-ache,

Soup beans, string beans, float-ing all a-round;
Cream puffs, ear-muffs, man-y to be found;

Silk hats, door-mats, bed slats, Dem-o-crats; Cow-bells, door-bells

beck-on you to dine; Meat-balls, fish balls,

moth-balls, can-non-balls. Come on in; the chow-der's fine!

MRS. MURPHY'S CHOWDER Words and Music by Oscar Brand. TRO - © 1961 (renewed) Hollis Music, Inc., New York, NY. Used by permission.

LISTENING CD 19:1

Brafferton Village/Walsh's Hornpipe

Irish Folk Music

Listen for the dance steps in this performance by
The Chieftains and Kathryn Tickell.

Seasonal Songs

This Korean folk song tells about the joyful coming of spring.

Sing this song with pitch syllables and hand signs.

Spring Has Come!

CD 19:2

Words by Chu Shik Ham
Music by Sol Chul Jang
English Words by Linda Worsley

Korean: 푸 른 바 다 건 너 서 봄 이 봄 - 이 와 요
Pronunciation: pu ɾən ba da gʌn nʌ sʌ bom i bom i wa yo
English: 1. Cross-ing o - ver blue o - cean, Spring,_ spring_ is com-ing!
2. O - ver field and high moun-tain, Spring,_ spring_ is com-ing,

제 비 앞 장 세 - 우 - 고 봄 이 봄 이 와 요
jɛ bi ab jang dɛ wu go bom i bom i wa yo
Fol-low-ing the lit-tle spar - row, Spring,_ spring is com-ing!
Fol-low-ing the lit-tle spar - row, Spring,_ spring is com-ing!

Use *World Instruments* **CD-ROM**
to learn more about Asian instruments.

May Day was first celebrated in Europe. It was a day of games and feasting that celebrated the end of winter and the return of the sun.

Find five notes moving up stepwise in "May Day Carol."

May Day Carol

CD 19:6

English Folk Song

1. I have been wan - d'ring all this___ night and
2. My song is done and I must be gone, no

some time of this day. And now re - turn - ing
long - er can I stay. So bless you all, both

home a - gain, I've brought you a branch of May.
great and small, and send you a joy - ful May.

CONCEPT
METER

SKILLS
SING

Earth Day is a day to remind people to look at the planet and decide what needs to be done to protect its beauty. This song is a reminder that the beauty of the earth is for everyone to enjoy.

Just Like the Sun

CD 19:9

Words and Music by Raffi
English Words by Linda Worsley

1. Just like the birds that keep on fly - ing,   Just like the
2. Just as the flow - ers keep on bloom-ing,   Just like the

wind that keeps on blow-ing,   I see a wave of o-ceans roll-ing
leaves that keep on turn-ing   I feel the change of sea-sons flow-ing

on and on,   Just like the   sun, these gifts are here for ev-ery-one.
on and on,   Just like the   sun, these gifts are here for ev-ery-one.

Just like the trees that keep on giv-ing, Just like the
Just like the moon that keeps on shin-ing, Just like the

grass that keeps on grow-ing, I hear the sound of chil-dren sing-ing
stars that keep on twink-ling, I know a world of won-ders play-ing

on and on, Just like the sun, these gifts are here for
on and on, Just like the

Go back to the beginning and sing to the end
(D.C. al Fine)

ev - ery - one. sun, these gifts are here for ev - ery-one.

Move with the beat as you sing the song.

Cinco de Mayo celebrates the victory of a small Mexican army over a large French army. Today people celebrate with dancing, music, and good things to eat. This song is about a sweet, warm drink made with corn.

El atole

The Atole

CD 19:12

Mexican Folk Song
Adapted by José-Luis Orozco
English Words by Linda Worsley

Spanish: Pa - sen a to - mar a - to - le,
Pronunciation: pa sen a to maɾ a to le
English: Come on in to drink a - to - le,

to - dos los que van pa - san - do, a - to - li - to cham - pu-
to ðos los ke βan pa san do a to li to cham pu
ev - 'ry-one that pass - es by here A - to - le with choc-o-late

rra - do, a - quí es-ta - mos sa - bo - rean - do.
ɾa ðo a kyes ta mos sa βo ɾean do
flav - 'ring is what we are now sa - vor - ing.

Pa - sen a co-mer ta - ma - les, to - dos los que van pa-
pa sen a ko meɾ ta ma les to ðos los ke βan pa
Come on in to eat ta - ma - les, ev - 'ry-one that pass - es

san - do,   ta - ma - li - tos ca - lien - ti - tos,
san   do   ta   ma   li   tos   ka   lyen   ti   tos
by   here.   Hot   and   spi - cy   fresh   ta - ma - les,

a - quí es - ta - mos dis - fru - tan - do.
a   kyes   ta   mos   dis   fru   tan   do
We   just   love   to   eat   ta - ma - les.

 LISTENING   CD 19:16

Los mariachis Mexican Folk Song

Mariachi music began in Mexico in the 1800s.
The instruments in mariachi groups are usually violins,
guitars, vihuelas, guitarrons, and trumpets.

 CD-ROM

Use *World Instruments* **CD-ROM** to learn more about Mexican instruments.

Playing the Recorder

C

D

E

F

F#

G

A

B♭

B

C'

D'

Glossary of Instruments

accordion a hand-held keyboard instrument that is played by pressing keys or buttons while air is forced through the instrument. It is often played while standing and held by straps over the shoulders, **CD 21:10**

bagpipe a member of the woodwind family that is played by blowing air through a tube into the bag and then pressing the bag so that the air is forced out through the pipes, **88 CD 21:11**

banjo a member of the string family that is played by plucking or strumming the strings, **31 CD 21:20**

bass drum a large member of the percussion family that gives a deep sound when hit, **CD 20:32**

bassoon a member of the woodwind family that is played by blowing into the reed while covering holes along the body with fingers, **CD 20:15**

cello the second-largest member of the string family in an orchestra, which is held between the knees and played by bowing or plucking the strings, **178 CD 20:6**

clarinet a member of the woodwind family that is played by blowing into the mouthpiece while covering holes along the body with fingers, **31 CD 20:12**

conga a percussion instrument used in Latin America that has a low-pitched sound when struck, **CD 21:30**

cymbal A dish-shaped percussion instrument that is often played by hitting one against another to make a clashing sound, **CD 20:37**

djembe a West African percussion instrument that is a drum made from pottery or wood and played with the hands, **CD 21:2**

double bass the largest instrument of the string family in an orchestra, which is held upright and played by bowing or plucking the strings, **CD 20:7**

flute a member of the woodwind family that is played by blowing across a hole at one end while covering holes along the body with fingers, **CD 20:10**

French horn a member of the brass family that is played by buzzing the lips into the mouthpiece while pressing keys with fingers, **CD 20:20**

güiro a Latin American percussion instrument that is made from a gourd and has a bumpy surface that is scraped with a stick to make a sound, **CD 21:33**

guitar a popular string instrument that is played by plucking or strumming the strings, **14** **CD 21:13**

harp one of the oldest instruments in the string family, played by plucking or strumming the strings with fingers, **CD 20:8**

koto a long, flat, Japanese string instrument that is played by plucking its 13 strings, **CD 21:53**

Glossary of Instruments   401

mandolin a member of the string family that is similar to a guitar, but it has a different body shape and 8 metal strings, **CD 21:16**

maracas Latin American percussion instruments played in pairs by shaking when held at the handles, **CD 21:35**

oboe a double-reed woodwind instrument that is played by blowing into the reed while covering holes along the body with fingers, **CD 20:13**

piano a percussion instrument that is played by pressing the keys on the keyboard, **155 CD 20:41**

piccolo one of the smaller members of the woodwind family that is a small flute that plays high pitches, **CD 20:11**

saxophone a member of the woodwind family that is played by blowing into the mouthpiece while pushing the keys along the body with fingers, **CD 20:16**

shekere an African percussion instrument that is a hollow gourd covered with a net of beads or seeds and is played by shaking, **CD 21:8**

slit drum
a percussion instrument used in Africa, Asia, and the South Pacific that is formed by hollowing a tree trunk through a slit on one side and played by hitting with sticks, **CD 21:9**

snare drum
a member of the percussion family that is played by hitting the top of the drum with drumsticks to vibrate wires along the bottom, **31 CD 20:35**

spoons a common object used as a percussion instrument by holding two together and hitting them against the body. Musicians often use special spoons fastened together with a wooden handle, **15 CD 21:23**

taiko drum
a barrel-shaped Japanese percussion instrument that is played with sticks, or *bachi*, **CD 21:51**

tambourine
a small, hand-held percussion instrument that has metal disks attached loosely around the rim and is played by shaking or hitting it with the hand, **31 CD 20:36**

timpani percussion instruments that are a set of large kettle-shaped drums, played with mallets and tuned to different pitches, **CD 20:26**

trombone a large, low-pitched member of the brass family, which is played by buzzing the lips into the mouthpiece while moving the slide in and out, **CD 20:21**

trumpet the smallest, highest-pitched member of the brass family, which is played by buzzing the lips into the mouthpiece while pressing keys with fingers, **CD 20:18**

tuba the largest, lowest-pitched member of the brass family, which is played by buzzing the lips into the mouthpiece while pressing keys with fingers, **CD 20:22**

viola a member of the string family slightly larger than the violin, which is held under the chin and played by bowing or plucking the strings, **CD 20:5**

violin the smallest member of the string family in an orchestra, which is held under the chin and played by bowing or plucking the strings, **31 CD 20:4**

xylophone a percussion instrument that is played by hitting the wooden bars with small wooden hammers, or mallets, **CD 20:30**

Glossary of Terms

A

accelerando gradually getting faster, **224**

accompaniment a musical background to a melody, **191**

allegro fast tempo, **67**

B

bar line (‖) a line that marks the end of a measure, **15**

beat the pulse felt in most music, **8**

C

canon a song form with two or more voices in which the melody is introduced and imitated one or more times; similar to a round, **141**

chord three or more pitches sounded together, **191**

choreographer a person who creates a pattern of dance movements to go with music, **112**

choreography a pattern of dance movements to go with specific music, **112**

D

coda a short section added to the end of a piece of music, **155**

conductor a person who leads performers using special patterns of arm movements, **106**

contrast combining one musical idea with a different one, **74**

countermelody a contrasting melody written to go with a song, **60**

D

dotted half note (𝅗𝅥.) a note equal to one half note plus one quarter note, **177**

downbeat the first beat of each measure, **170**

downstage the space on the stage closest to the audience, **291**

dynamics the loudness or softness of music, **63**

E

eighth notes (♫) musical notes that show two sounds to a beat, **15**

eighth rest (❼) a rest that lasts on half of a beat, **223**

F

first ending (|1. ____) a sign that tells you to go back to the beginning of the song and sing to the second ending, **100**

form the order of phrases or sections, or the plan, of a piece of music, **46**

forte (*f*) loud, **63**

H

half note (♩) a note that shows a sound that is two beats long, **58**

harmony two or more pitches sung or played at the same time, **192**

high *do* the pitch one octave higher than the *do* that begins the scale, **139**

I

identical exactly the same, **128**

interlude a short musical connection between sections or verses of a song, **152**

L

largo slow tempo, **67**

leap one way a melody moves; to move higher or lower by jumping over two or more pitches, **148**

legato smooth and connected, **226**

limerick a funny, five-line rhyming poem, **234**

low *la* the pitch *la* that lies below *do*, **98**

low *so* the pitch *so* that lies below *do*, **98**

M

measure a unit used to group notes and rests, **15**

melody a pattern of pitches that moves upward, downward, or stays the same; a tune, **12**

meter the pattern of beats grouped in a measure of music, **106**

meter signature the symbol that tells how many beats are grouped in each measure and what kind of note equals one beat, **15**

O

ostinato a musical pattern that repeats over and over, **131**

P

pentatonic a scale having only five pitches, **140**

phrase a short section of music that is one musical thought, **91**

piano (*p*) soft, **63**

pitch how high or low a sound is, **12**

pizzicato played by plucking a stringed instrument, **228**

Q

quarter note (♩) the symbol for one sound to a beat, **15**

quarter rest (𝄽) a symbol for silence the length of one quarter note, **15**

R

refrain a section of a song that is repeated after each verse, **91**

repeat sign (:‖) a symbol that tells you to repeat part of a piece of music, **96**

repetition using the same musical idea more than once, **74**

rhythm combinations of longer and shorter sounds and silences, **9**

rondo a piece of music in which the A section always returns, with different sections in between, such as ABACA, **155**

round a type of canon; a short song for three or more voices in which each voice begins at a different time, **141**

S

samba a Brazilian dance that has its own special movements, **111**

scale a group of pitches in order from lowest to highest, **140**

second ending (‖2.⸻) the ending after the first ending of a song, **100**

similar having many but not all qualities the same, **128**

sixteenth note (♪) four notes that equal one beat, **136**

skip one way a melody moves; to move higher or lower by jumping over a pitch, **148**

spiritual an African American folk song, many of which began as religious songs, **324**

staccato short and choppy, **226**

staff the five lines and four spaces on which musical notes are written, **20**

stage left the space to the left of the actor when facing the audience, **291**

stage right the space to the right of the actor when facing the audience, **291**

step one way a melody moves; to move higher or lower to the next pitch, **148**

T

tempo the speed of the beat, **66**

tie (⌢ or ⌣) a curved line that connects two notes of the same pitch and means that the sound should be held for the length of both notes, **70**

tonal center the home tone or pitch around which a melody seems to center; often the last pitch, **206**

tone color the special sound of each instrument or voice, **26**

treble clef or **G clef** ( ) tells that the notes on the second line of a staff are called G, **187**

U

unison all instruments or voices playing or singing the same notes at the same time, **141**

upbeat the last beat of each measure, **170**

upstage the space on the stage farthest away from the audience, **291**

V

verse a section of a song that is repeated using the same melody but different words, **91**

W

whole note ( ) a note to show a sound that lasts four beats, **180**

whole rest (━) a rest to show a silence that lasts four beats, **180**

Look High, Look Low, Words and Music by John Jacobson and John Higgins. Copyright © 2002 by HAL LEONARD CORPORATION. International Copyright Secured. All Rights Reserved.

Marvelous Toy, The, Words and Music by Tom Paxton. Copyright © 1961. Renewed 1989. Pax Music (ASCAP) and DreamWorks Songs (ASCAP). Worldwide Rights for Pax Music and DreamWorks Songs Administered by Cherry Lane Music Publishing Company, Inc. International Copyright Secured. All Rights Reserved.

Minuteman Minute Song, The, from THE PATRIOTS. Words and Music by Mary Lynn Lightfoot and Lee Brandon. Copyright © 1993 by Heritage Music Press (a division of The Lorenz Corporation). International Copyright Secured. All Rights Reserved.

Moon and Me by Bill Harley. © 1988 Round River Music/Bill Harley. All Rights Reserved Used by Permission. www.billharley.com.

Movin' Right Along by Paul Williams and Kenneth L. Ascher. Copyright © 1979 Jim Henson Productions, Inc. All Rights Administered by Sony/ATV Music Publishing, 8 Music Square West, Nashville, TN 37203. International Copyright Secured. All Rights Reserved.

Mrs. Murphy's Chowder, Based on an Irish Folk Song, New words and music arrangement by Oscar Brand. TRO - © Copyright 1961 (Renewed) Hollis Music, Inc., New York, NY. International Copyright Secured. All Rights Reserved Including Public Performance For Profit. Used by Permission.

Music of the World A-Turnin', Words and Music by Estelle Levitt and Don Thomas. Copyright © 1965 (Renewed 1993). EMI BLACKWOOD MUSIC INC. All Rights Reserved. International Copyright Secured. Used by Permission.

My Friend Tom, Words and Music by John Jacobson and Alan Billingsley. Copyright © 2002 by HAL LEONARD CORPORATION. International Copyright Secured. All Rights Reserved.

One Small Voice, from the Television Series SESAME STREET. Words and Music by Jeff Moss. Copyright © 1989 Festival Attractions, Inc. International Copyright Secured. All Rights Reserved.

Out from the Wilderness, Music Attributed To J. Warner. Words by Robert Quackenbush. Copyright © by Lothrop, Lee & Shepard Books, a div. of William Morrow & Co., Inc. International Copyright Secured. All Rights Reserved.

Pat-A-Pan, Original Words and Music by Bernard de la Monnoye. English Words by Merrill Staton. Copyright © 1987 by Rockhaven Music. International Copyright Secured. All Rights Reserved.

Preamble, The, From MTI's Broadway Junior Broadway for Kids SCHOOLHOUSE ROCK LIVE! Junior. Music and Lyrics by Lynn Ahrens. Copyright © Music and Lyrics 1995 and TM American Broadcasting Companies, Inc. The above copyright notice may be subject to change to conform to new or different requirements upon written notification from American Broadcasting Companies, Inc. All Rights Reserved. Used by Permission.

Rainbow Connection,The, Words and Music by Paul Williams and Kenneth L.Ascher. Copyright © 1979. Jim Henson Productions, Inc. All Rights Administered by Sony/ATV Music Publishing, 8 Music Square West, Nashville, TN 37203. International Copyright Secured. All Rights Reserved.

Recycle Rap, Words and Music by Teresa Jennings. Copyright © 1990 by Plank Road Publishing. International Copyright Secured. All Rights Reserved.

Shoo Fly Pie and Apple Pan Dowdy, Lyrics by Sammy Gallop. Music by Guy Wood. Copyright © 1945. CAPITOL SONGS, INC. © Renewed 1973. WAROCK CORP. and SAMMY GALLOP MUSIC COMPANY. All Rights Reserved.

Simon Says, Words and Music by Elliot Chiprut. Copyright © Super Bubble Music Corp. International Copyright Secured. All Rights Reserved.

Spiders by Mary Ann Hoberman, from *Bugs*. Copyright © 1976. The Viking Press. All Rights Reserved.

Step into the Spotlight, Words and Music by Emily Crocker, John Higgins and John Jacobson. Copyright © 2004 by HAL LEONARD COR-PORATION. International Copyright Secured. All Rights Reserved.

Texas, Our Texas, Words by Gladys Yoakum Wright and William J. Marsh. Music by William J. Marsh. Copyright © 1925 by William J. Marsh. Copyright renewed 1953 by William J. Marsh. Used by Permission of Owen E. Thomas and Mary C. Hearne, Copyright owners. Published by Southern Music Company.

This Is America, Words and Music by Teresa Jennings. Copyright © 2002 by Plank Road Publishing. International Copyright Secured. All Rights Reserved.

This a Way and That a Way, Words and Music by John Jacobson and Alan Billingsley. Copyright © 1997 by HAL LEONARD CORPORATION. International Copyright Secured. All Rights Reserved.

This Land is Your Land, Words and Music by Woody Guthrie. TRO - © Copyright 1956. Renewed 1958. Renewed 1970. Renewed 1972. Renewed. Ludlow Music, Inc., New York, NY. International Copyright Secured. All Rights Reserved Including Public Performance For Profit. Used by Permission.

Three Is a Magic Number, From MTI's Broadway Junior Broadway for Kids SCHOOLHOUSE ROCK LIVE! Junior. Music and Lyrics by Bob Dorough. Copyright © Music and Lyrics 1995 and TM American Broadcasting Companies, Inc. The above copyright notice may be subject to change to conform to new or different requirements upon written notification from American Broadcasting Companies, Inc. All Rights Reserved. Used by Permission. Used by Permission.

Three Little Birds, Words and Music by Bob Marley. Copyright © 1977. Fifty-Six Hope Road Music, Ltd., Odnil Music, Ltd. and Blue Mountain Music, Ltd. All Rights for the United States and Canada Controlled and Administered by Fairwood Music USA. International Copyright Secured. All Rights Reserved.

Treasure Chests, Words and Music by Minnie O'Leary. Copyright © 1981 by Tom O'Leary. International Copyright Secured. All Rights Reserved.

Ujamaa, from KWANZAA SUITE. Words and Music by Stan Spottswood. Copyright © 2002. Stan Spottswood/World Music Press (ASCAP). World Music Press, P.O. Box 2565, Danbury, CT 06813-2565. www.worldmusicpress.com. All Rights Reserved.

When I First Came to This Land, Words and Music by Oscar Brand. TRO - © Copyright 1957. Renewed 1965, Renewed. Ludlow Music, Inc., New York, NY. International Copyright Secured. All Rights Reserved Including Public Performance For Profit. Used by Permission.

Yellow Submarine, Words and Music by John Lennon and Paul McCartney. Copyright © 1966. Sony/ATV Songs LLC. Copyright Renewed. All Rights Administered by Sony/ATV Music Publishing, 8 Music Square West, Nashville, TN 37203. International Copyright Secured. All Rights Reserved.

Apple Tree by Katalin Forrai, from *Music in Preschool*. Copyright © 1985 Translated and adapted by Jean Sinor. Copyright © Katalin Forrai, 1974, 1988; Jean Sinor, 1988. 1st and 2nd editions in English published by CORVINA, Budapest. 3rd edition published by KULTA Foreign Trading Co. Budapest, 1995.

City Music by Tony Mitton. Copyright © 1997 by Tony Mitton. Reprinted by Permission of Murray Pollinger Literary Agent. Reprinted in *Poems Go Clang! A Collection of Noisy Verse*. Text Copyright © 1997. All Rights Reserved.

Hope by Emily Dickinson, from *The Complete Poems of Emily Dickinson*. Copyright © 1960. Edited by Thomas H. Johnson. Little, Brown and Company. All Rights Reserved.

I Raised a Great Hullabaloo, anonymous. Reprinted in *The Random House Book of Poetry For Children*. Selected and introduced by Jack Prelutsky. Copyright © 1983 by Random House, Inc. All Rights Reserved.

Isabella and the Troll, Originally The Singing Sack, from *The Singing Sack: 28 Song-Stories from Around the World*. Compilation Copyright ©1989. A & C Black, Ltd. London. All Rights Reserved.

I Woke Up in the Morning by Sonja Dunn and Lou Pamenter, from *Butterscotch Dreams*. Copyright © 1987 by Sonja Dunn and Lou Pamenter. Pembroke Publishers Ltd. All Rights Reserved.

Lincoln by Myra Cohn Livingston, from *Remembering and Other Poems*. Copyright © 1989 by Myra Cohn Livingston. Margaret K. McElderry Books, The Macmillan Publishing Company. All Rights Reserved.

Night by Sara Teasdale, from *Stars To-night*. Copyright © 1930. Macmillan. Reprinted in *Anthology of Children's Literature*, 5th Edition, Houghton Mifflin Company. Copyright © 1970, 1977. All Rights Reserved. Used by Permission.

Our Washing Machine by Patricia Hubbell, from *The Apple Vendor's Fair*. Copyright © 1963, 1991. Atheneum. Reprinted by Permission of Maria Reiner for the author in *Poems Go Clang! A Collection of Noisy Verse*. Text Copyright © 1963, 1991. All Rights Reserved.

There Was An Old Lady by Dennis Lee, from *Poem Stew*. Selected by William Cole. Copyright © 1981. Copyright by Dennis Lee. HarperTrophy, A Division of HarperCollins Publishers. All Rights Reserved. Used by Permission.

Way Down South, anonymous. Reprinted in *The Random House Book of Poetry For Children*. Selected and introduced by Jack Prelutsky. Copyright © 1983 by Random House, Inc. All Rights Reserved.

CREDITS

Illustration Credits: Barry Ablett: 342-343. Ann Barrow:128, 129. Rose Mary Berlin: 63. Kristin Barr: v, Spotlight on Reading (2). Delana Bettoli: 216-217. Blair Bostick: 138, 139. Ka Botzis: 28-29. Vicki Bradley: 8 –9. S.G. Brooks: 365. Priscilla Burris: 204-205. Carlos Caban: 87. Gina Capaldi: 132, 133. Carly Castillon: 186-187. Antonio Castro: 305. Emilie Chollat: 104, 105. Peter Church: iv, 312, Spotlight on Concepts (2). Jack Crane: 116. Carolyn Croll: 272. Renee Daily: 48-49, 60-61 Billy Davis: 1, Spotlight on Celebrations (2). Nancy Davis: 136, 136-137. Viviana M. Diaz: 318-319. Sarah Dillard: 225. Robert Dombrowski: 310-311. Bob Doucet: 306-307. Leslie Evans: 152-153. Peter Fasolino: 346, 347, 348. Jeff Fillbach: 244. Ruth Flanigan: 366-367. Andrea Gabriel: 56-57. J.D. Gentry: 264. Justin Gerard: 94. Mariano Gil: 78,79. Renee Graef: vi, Spotlight on Performance (2). Diane Greenseid: 320-321. Gershom Griffith: 148-149. Mizue Ono Hamilton: 103. Yu-Mei Han: 222-223. Judy Hand: 112-113. Amanda Harvey: 332-333, 336-337, 338, 340. Linda Howard Bittner: 344, 345. Tim Jones: 326. Fiona King: 176-177, 330, 331. Diana Kizlauskas: 58-59. Loretta Krupinski: 226. Fran Lee: 12-13. Laura Logan: 96-97, 100-101. Katherine Lucas: 234-235. Loretta Lustig: 170-171. Stephen Marchesi: 47. Erin Mauterer: 106-107. Deborah Maze: 393. Sue Mell: 359. Elise Mills: 220-221. Carol Newsom: 206-207, 263. Tim Nihoff: 74, 76-77. Cheryl Kirk Noll: 146-147. Laurie O'Keefe: 53. Ed Olson: 64. Rik Olson: 260-261. Kathleen O'Malley: 90, 273. David Opie: 6-7. Frank Ordaz: 249. John Perlock: 192-193. Tamara Petrosino: 385. Gary R. Phillips: 140-141. Ilene Richard: 243. Cecile Schoberle: 24, 24-25. Stacey Schuett: 248-249. Wendy Smith-Griswold: 316. Dick Smolinski: 208-209, 245. Craig Spearing: 72-73. Bridget Starr Taylor: 68-69. Judy Stead: 258. Thomas Stefflbauer: 349, 350, 351. Lydia Taranovic: 246, 246-247. Mary Teichman: 66-67. Jeremy Tugeau: 250. Neecy Twinem: 76-77. Lin Wang: 324. Laura Watson: 308-309. Paula Wendland: 322, 323. Elizabeth Wolf: 154-155. Jason Wolff: 11, 254-255. Nicole E. Wong: 314-315.

All photographs are copyright of Macmillan/McGraw-Hill (MMH) except as noted below.

Allan Landau for MMH: iv-vii: t.r., 2-3: c., 3: l., 4: b., 5: b., 6: c.l., c., c.r., 11: t.l., t.r., 15: b.r., 35: l., c.l., c., c.r., r., 37: b.l., b.c., b.r., 38: c., 54: c., 55: 1., 2., 3., 4., 5., 70: t.c.l., 91: t., c., 93: b.l., 162-163: r., 202-203: bkgd., 204: b.l., 212: 1., 2., 3., 4., 306: b., 403: t.c.l., b.l., 404: t.l. Jade Albert for MMH: cover, i: b.r. Shane Morgan for MMH: 85: b.r., b.l., b.c., 89: l., 178: b., 378: t., t.r., 379: t., 387: b.r. iv-vii: t.c., b.l., t.l., t.c.l., l., b.l., b.c.l., b.c.r., b.c. PhotoDisc, Inc.; b.r., t.r., c.r. Corbis.

iv-vii: cowbell, frame drum, saxophone, congas, electric keyboard, tuba, wood blocks, Chinese wood blocks, side drum, trumpet, PhotoDisc, Inc.; French horn, decorated drum, silver drum, trumpet, PhotoDisc, Inc.; r. Michael Dwyer/AP/Wide World Photos; border, flag, Richard Cummins/Corbis; border, map, Cartesia/ PhotoDisc, Inc./Getty Images; border, rabbit, Darrell Gulin/ Corbis; border, hat and boots, Jules Frazier/PhotoDisc, Inc./ Getty Images; border, mission, Andre Jenny/Alamy Images, Ltd. A-B: border, bkgd. PhotoDisc, Inc. B: t.l: Jim Mosenfelder/ ImageDirect/Getty Images; t.r. Derick A. Thomas, Dat's Jazz/Corbis; b.l. Richard Cummins/Corbis; b.r. Jonathan A. Nourok/PhotoEdit, Inc.; border, derricks, cactus, PhotoDisc, Inc/; border, bird, Jeremy Woodhouse/PhotoDisc, Inc./Getty Images; border, bridge, Corbis. C: border, flag, The Granger Collection, New York. C-D: border, cactus, PhotoDisc, Inc.; border, hat and boots, Jules Frazier/PhotoDisc, Inc./Getty Images. D: border, flag, The Granger Collection, New York. E: t.r. Texas Secretary of State; t.l. The Granger Collection, New York; b.l.t: D. Robert & Lorri Franz/Corbis; c.r. Animals Animals/Earth Scenes; b.r. Corbis; border, flag, Richard Cummins/ Corbis; border, map, Cartesia/PhotoDisc, Inc./Getty Images; border, rabbit, Darrell Gulin/Corbis; border, hat and boots, Jules Frazier/PhotoDisc, Inc./Getty Images; border, mission, Andre Jenny/Alamy Images, Ltd. E-F: bkgd. Lindsay Hebberd/ Corbis; border, bkgd. PhotoDisc, Inc. F: t.r. Animals Animals/ Earth Scenes; b.l. Rosemary Calvert/Stone/Getty Images; border, derricks, cactus, PhotoDisc, Inc.; border, bridge, Corbis. G: border, riverwalk, PhotoDisc, Inc.; border, children, Bettmann/Corbis; border, mission, Andre Jenny/Alamy Images, Ltd.; border, flag, The Granger Collection, New York. G-H: border, storm, Hulton Archive/Getty Images. H: t. Richard Cummins/Corbis; b. Tom Algire/SuperStock; border, derricks, PhotoDisc, Inc.; border, engraving, MPI/Hulton Archive/Getty Images; border, rocks, David Muench/Corbis. I: t.l. Bettmann/ Corbis; c. A. G. Hamel/Corbis; b.l. David R. Frazier Photo Library; b.r. Dave G. Houser/Corbis; border, dome, G. E. Kidder Smith/Corbis; border, Alamo, Kean Collection/Hulton Archive/Getty Images. I-J: l. Bettmann/Corbis; border, dam, Underwood & Underwood/Corbis; border, oil field, H. P. Meissner/Hulton Archive/Getty Images. J: t.r. Hot Ideas/Index Stock Imagery; t.c. J. Purdy/Corbis; b.l. Bettmann/Corbis; b.r. AP Photo; c.r. Corbis; border, gusher, factory, Hulton Archive/ Getty Images. K: t.l. Steve Terrill/Corbis; t.r. David Stoecklein/ Corbis; border, dome, G. E. Kidder Smith/Corbis; border, Alamo, Kean Collection/Hulton Archive/Getty Images. K-L: border, dam, Underwood & Underwood/Corbis; border, oil field, H. P. Meissner/Hulton Archive/Getty Images. L: t. Jonathan Blair/Corbis; border, gusher, factory, Hulton Archive/ Getty Images. M: b. George H. H. Huey/Corbis. M-N: c. Corbis; border, peppers, flag, maracas, PhotoDisc, Inc.; border, piñata, Image Club; border, taco, Comstock. N: b.l. Danny Lehman/ Corbis; t.r. Amado Peña/Peña Studio Gallery. O-P: c. Bob Daemmrich Photography; border, peppers, flag, maracas, PhotoDisc, Inc.; border, piñata, Image Club; border, taco, Comstock. P: r. Philip Gould/Corbis. Q: b. Jonathan Blair/ Corbis; t.r. Danny Lehman/Corbis; c., border, riverwalk, PhotoDisc, Inc.; border, children, Bettmann/Corbis; border, mission, Andre Jenny/Alamy Images, Ltd.; border, flag, The Granger Collection, New York; Q-R: bkgd. PhotoDisc, Inc.; border, storm, Hulton Archive/Getty Images. R: t.r., c.r., b.r. Joe McDonald/Corbis; t.l. Bo Zaunders/Corbis; c.l. Danny Lehman/ Corbis; bkgd. PhotoDisc, Inc.; bkgd. MPI/Hulton Archive/Getty

Images; bkgd. David Muench/Corbis. S: border, flag, The Granger Collection, New York. S-T: t. Lindsay Hebberd/Corbis; border, cactus, PhotoDisc, Inc.; border, hat and boots, Jules Frazier/PhotoDisc, Inc.; border, flag, T: Peña Studios/ courtesy of Amado Peña Gallery; border, flag, The Granger Collection, New York. U: t. David Muench/Stone/Getty Images; inset, Corbis; border, flag, The Granger Collection, New York. U-V: border, cactus, PhotoDisc, Inc.; border, hat and boots, Jules Frazier/PhotoDisc, Inc./Getty Images. V: r. Bettmann/ Corbis; bkgd. David Muench/Corbis; border, flag, The Granger Collection, New Yrok. W: border, flag, Richard Cummins/ Corbis; border, map, Cartesia/PhotoDisc, Inc./Getty Images; border, rabbit, Darrell Gulin/Corbis; border, hat and boots, Jules Frazier/PhotoDisc, Inc./Getty Images; border, mission, Andre Jenny/Alamy Images, Ltd.; border, bridge, Corbis; x., bkgd. Bob Daemmrich/PhotoEdit, Inc.; border, bkgd. PhotoDisc, Inc. X: b.l. Kevin Winter/Getty Images; t. Robert Landau/Corbis; border, derricks, cactus, PhotoDisc, Inc.; border, bird, Jeremy Woodhouse/PhotoDisc, Inc./Getty Images; border, bridge, Corbis; b.r. Bob Daemmrich/ Bob Daemmrich Photography. 6-7: t. MetaCreations/Kai Power Photos. 8-9: t. MetaCreations/Kai Power Photos. 10-11: bkgd. MetaCreations/Kai Power Photos. 12: c. Photodisc Green/ Getty Images. 13: bkgd. MetaCreations/Kai Power Photos. 14: b.r. Bettmann/Corbis. 14-15: t. Corel. 15: t.r. PhotoDisc, Inc. 16-17: bkgd. Photodisc Green/Getty Images; t. Corel. 18-19: bkgd. Corbis. 20: b. R.W. Jones/Corbis. 20-21: bkgd. Corel. 21: t.r. Tony Freeman/PhotoEdit, Inc. 22: bkgd. Corel. 23: bkgd. Corel. 24: t.r. Artville, LLC. 25: t. Fine Arts in Hungary/Hungarian National Gallery; b.r., c.r. Artville, LLC. 26: c.r. Popperfoto/Alamy Images, Ltd. 26-27: t. Corel. 30: b. Argenphoto/Stock SudamÉrica; c.l. Jacques Jangoux/Alamy Images, Ltd.; t. Nik Wheeler/Corbis. 30-31: bkgd. Francesco Venturi/Corbis. 31: t.c., c. Corbis; c.l., c.r. PhotoDisc, Inc.; b.r. MarKamusic. 32: b. Craig Lovell/Corbis. 32-33: bkgd. Francesco Venturi/Corbis. 33: b.l.t. Haydee Mendizabal/Images of Eyes Gallery; t.r. Suzanne Murphy-Larronde/Suzanne Murphy-Larronde Photography; c.r. MarKamusic. 34-35: bkgd., t. Charles O'Rear/Corbis. 35: b.l. Lynn Goldsmith/Corbis. 36: c.l. Louise Gubb/The Image Works; c.r. Carol Beckwith & Angela Fisher/HAGA/The Image Works. 36-37: t., bkgd. Charles O'Rear/Corbis. 37: t.r. PhotoDisc, Inc. 40: t. Corbis. 41: b.r. PhotoDisc, Inc. 42-43: t. Steve Satushek/Image Bank/Getty Images; b. Jamie Marcial/SuperStock. 43: t.r. Roy Ooms/ Masterfile; t.r. Taxi/Getty Images. 44: t. Chuck Keeler, Jr./Corbis; b.l. James Urbach/Superstock. 45: b. Ariel Skelley/ Corbis; t.r. Jeffrey W. Myers/Corbis. 46-47: bkgd. PhotoDisc, Inc.; M. Angelo/Corbis. 50: l. Carnegie Museum of Natural History; t. The Granger Collection; t.r. Mike Greenlar/ The Image Works, Inc. 50-51: b. Rufus Grider/Newberry Library, Chicago/SuperStock. 51: b. Carnegie Museum of Natural History; t.r., Marilyn "Angel" Wynn/Nativestock.com; b.l. Getty Images. 52: t.r. Mike Okoniewski-New York State Fair/HO/AP/Wide World Photos; b.l. AP/Wide World Photos; c.r. Marilyn "Angel" Wynn/Nativestock.com. 52-53: t. Rufus Grider/Newberry Library, Chicago/SuperStock. 54: l. PhotoDisc, Inc. 54-55: bkgd. Corel. 55: t.r., b. PhotoDisc, Inc. 62-63: bkgd. NASA. 64: t. Scala/Art Resource, NY. 64-65: bkgd. Corbis. 66: t. Fukuhara, Inc./Corbis. 67: l. PhotoDisc, Inc.; t. Fukuhara, Inc./Corbis. 68: t. Fukuhara, Inc./Corbis. 69: t. Fukuhara, Inc./Corbis. 70-71: bkgd. Sandro Vannini/Corbis. 71: t. Ted Spiegel/Corbis; b. Sandro Vannini/Corbis. 78: t.r. PhotoDisc, Inc. 80: t.r. PhotoDisc, Inc. 82-83: c. Bruce Forster/ Annie Griffiths Belt/Corbis. 86: b. Lawrence Migdale/Stock Boston, Inc./PictureQuest; c.r. David Grossman/The Image Works; c.l. Hinata Haga/HAGA/The Image Works; b. Corel. 88: t. Topham Picture Point/The Image Works, Inc. 89: r. Yann Layma/Stone Getty Images. 90-91: c. Corel. 92: b. The Thomas Collection/Art Gallery of Ontario; t.r. Nik Wheeler/Corbis. 93: r. Artville, LLC. 94-95: t. Image Farm Graphics. 96: t.r. Lebrecht Music & Arts Photo Library; t. Image Farm Graphics. 96-97: bkgd. Corel. 98: b. The Granger Collection. 98-99: bkgd. MetaCreations/Kai Power Photos. 98-101: t. MetaCreations/Kai Power Photos. 102: t.l. James Marshal/The Image Works; l., b. Ariadne Van Zandbergen/Lonely Planet Images. 102-103: bkgd. Christine Osborne/Corbis. 103: t. Penny Tweedie/Corbis. 104: b. Ariadne Van Zandbergen/Lonely Planet Images. 106: l. G. Anderhub/Lebrecht Music & Arts Photo Library; bkgd. PhotoDisc, Inc. 108: b. Jon Lusk/Redferns Music Picture Library. 108-109: c. JM Enternational/Redferns Music Picture Library; bkgd. PhotoDisc, Inc. 109: t.r. E. Comesana/Lebrecht Music & Arts Photo Library. 110: bkgd. Macduff Everton/The Image Works, Inc. 110-113: t. Corel. 111: c.r., b. MetaCreations/Kai Power Photos. 112-113: bkgd. Corel. 113: b.r. Mark Richards/ PhotoEdit, Inc. 114-115: bkgd. Andre Jenny/Alamy.com. 114-117: t. MetaCreations/Kai Power Photos. 115: c.r. Gary Bell/ImageState/Alamy.com. 117: r. Image Club Graphics. 121: c.r. Lebrecht Music & Arts Photo Library. 122-123: c. Corbis; l. Diane Meyer. 123: t. David Young-Wolff/PhotoEdit, Inc. 124: c.l., b.l. PhotoDisc, Inc. 125: b., r. PhotoDisc, Inc. 126: b. Stephanie Maze/Corbis. 126-127: bkgd. Corel; t.c. PhotoDisc, Inc. 126-129: t. Corel. 128-129: bkgd. Corel. 130: c. Grandma Moses Properties Co./Edward Owen/Art Resource, NY. 130-131: bkgd. Corbis. 132-133: bkgd. PhotoDisc, Inc. 134: c. Erich Lessing/Art Resource, NY; bkgd. James A. Sugar/ National Geographic Image Collection. 134-137: t. Corel. 135: bkgd. James A. Sugar/National Geographic Image Collection. 138: c. Corel. 138-141: bkgd. Corel. 142: c.l. Werner Forman/Art Resource, NY. 142-143: b. Arnulf Husmo/ Stone/Getty Images.; c., bkgd., t. Richard T. Nowitz/Corbis. 143: c. Sogne Fjord, Norway, Normann, Adelsteen (1848-1918)/Bonhams, London, UK/www.bridgeman.co.uk. 144: t. Masakatsu Yamazaki/HAGA/The Image Works. 144-145: c., bkgd., t. Richard T. Nowitz/Corbis. 145: c.r. The British Museum/Topham-HIP/The Image Works. 146: b.r. David Allen Brandt/Stone/Getty Images. 147: t. courtesy of Sonor Instruments, a division of Hohner, HSS. 150: c. Kevin Fleming/Corbis; c.r. PhotoDisc, Inc.; b. Corel. 150-151: bkgd. Corel. 150-153: t. Corel. 151: b.r. Hampton University

Museum, Virginia. 155: t.r. Reproduced by permission of The State Hermitage Museum, St. Petersburg, Russia/Corbis; b.r. Bettman/Corbis. 156-157: bkgd. Danny Lehman/Corbis. 159: t.r. PhotoDisc, Inc.; b.r. Photodisc Green/Getty Images. 161: b.r. PhotoDisc, Inc. 164: b.l. PhotoDisc, Inc. 165: c.r. PhotoDisc, Inc.; t. Corbis; b.l. PhotoDisc, Inc. 166-167: bkgd. Philip Coblentz/Brand X Pictures. 166-169: t. NASA. 168: t. National Gallery Collection/Corbis. 168-169: bkgd. Corbis. 172-173: bkgd. John and Lisa Merrill/Corbis. 173: b.r. Hubert Stadler/Corbis; t.r. Hans Georg Roth/Corbis. 175: c.r. Werner Forman/Art Resource, NY; t.r. Blaine Harrington/Corbis; b. Bill Ross/Corbis; r. Adam Woolfitt/Woodfin Camp & Associates. 177: t. Corbis; c., b. courtesy of Sonor Instruments, a division of Hohner, HSS. 178: c.r. Bettmann/Corbis. 178-179: bkgd. Bruce Forster/Stone/Getty Images. 178-181: t. Corel. 180-181: bkgd. Corbis. 182-183: t. Werner Forman Archive, Ltd./Art Resource, Inc.; r. MetaCreations/Kai Power Photos; bkgd. PhotoDisc, Inc. 183: c.r., t.r. Artville, LLC; r. Rube Goldberg, Inc. 184-185: bkgd. Enis Waugh/Stone/Getty Images; t. Werner Forman Archive, Ltd./Art Resource, NY. 185: t. PhotoDisc, Inc.; b.c., b.r. David Ball/Index Stock Imagery; b.l. British Museum, London, UK/Bridgeman Art Library. 186-189: t. Corel. 188: c. Robert Landau/Corbis. 188-189: bkgd. Macduff Everton/Image Bank/Getty Images. 189: b. Photodisc Blue/Getty Images; r. Peter Turnley/Corbis. 190-191: bkgd. PhotoDisc, Inc. 191: c.r. Keren Su/Corbis; t.r. Snark/Art Resource, Inc. 194: inset, Scott Bauer/USDA-ARS/University of Kentucky. 194-195: bkgd. K. Pomper/University of Kentucky. 196-197: bkgd. Ben Mangor/ SuperStock. 198: b.r. PhotoDisc, Inc. 200: t. PhotoDisc, Inc. 206-207: t. MetaCreations/Kai Power Photos. 208-209: t. MetaCreations/Kai Power Photos. 210-211: b. Morton Beebe/Corbis. 211: t.r. Gianni Dagli Orti/Corbis. 212: t.r. Bob Krist/Corbis. 212-213: bkgd. Macduff Everton/Corbis. 213: c. Schalkwijk/Art Resource, NY. 214-215: bkgd. Focus; t. Corbis. 215: c. Jeremy Horner/Corbis; t.r. Dean Conger/Corbis; c.r. PhotoDisc, Inc. 216-217: t. Corbis. 218-219: bkgd. MetaCreations/Kai Power Photos. 219: b. ASAP, Ltd./Index Stock Imagery. 224: t. Image Club Graphics. 225: t. Lebrecht Music & Arts Photo Library. 226-227: t. MetaTools. 228: t. Corbis; b.l. David Young-Wolff/PhotoEdit, Inc. 228-229: t. MetaTools. 229: t.r. Corbis. 230-231: bkgd. Peter Adams/ Alamy.com. 231: t. Art Resource, NY; b. Richard Romero/Tyba/ BrazilPhotos. 233: t.r. Michael J. Doolittle/The Image Works, Inc. 234-235: t. PhotoDisc, Inc. 236: t.r. Russell Gordon/Aurora Photos. 236-237: t. PhotoDisc, Inc.; bkgd. Steve Vidler/ SuperStock. 242: bkgd. PhotoDisc, Inc. 243: b.l. PhotoDisc, Inc. 247: t.r. PhotoDisc, Inc. 248: l. PhotoDisc, Inc. 250: b.l. Comstock. 251: t.c. Fine Art Photographic Library, London/Art Resource, NY. 252: l. MetaCreations/Kai Power Photos. 252-253: t. Bettmann/Corbis. 254: r., b.r. Bettman Archive/Corbis. 257: l. Comstock. 259: t., b.l. PhotoDisc, Inc. 262: c.l. Comstock. 264: t.r. Artville. 265: t. PhotoDisc, Inc. 268: l. Comstock. 269: b. Artville. 270: b. PhotoDisc, Inc. 271: b.r. Bridgeman Art Library. 274: t. Corbis. 278: t.r. PhotoDisc, Inc.; b. Corbis. 280: t.l., b.l., r. PhotoDisc, Inc. 281: t. PhotoDisc, Inc. 282: t.r., l. MetaCreations/Kai Power Photos. 283: b. PhotoDisc, Inc. 285: l. Erich Lessing/Art Resource, NY. 290: b. MTI; b.l. Corel. 291: c.r. Artville, LLC. 292: r. Artville, LLC. 293: t. Image Club Graphics. 295: c., b. MTI; PhotoDisc, Inc. 296: t. PhotoDisc, Inc. 300: t.l. PhotoDisc, Inc. 302: b. MTI. 303: b. PhotoDisc Green/Getty Images. 307: t.r. PhotoDisc, Inc. 309: t.r. PhotoDisc, Inc. 311: t.r. PhotoDisc, Inc. 313: b. 20th Century Fox/The Kobal Collection; t.r. PhotoDisc, Inc. 315: t.r. PhotoDisc, Inc. 317: t.r., b. 2001 Roger Ide Photography; t.r. PhotoDisc, Inc. 319: t.r. PhotoDisc, Inc. 321: t.r. PhotoDisc, Inc. 323: t.r. PhotoDisc, Inc. 325: c.r. Visuals Unlimited, Inc.; t.r. PhotoDisc, Inc. 327: c.r. SuperStock, Inc.; t.r. PhotoDisc, Inc. 328: t.r. NASA. 329: t.r. PhotoDisc, Inc. 331: b.r. Harold Wood; t.r. PhotoDisc, Inc. 333: t.r. PhotoDisc, Inc. 334: r. Kobal Collection. 335: t.r. Comstock. 337: t.r. Comstock. 339: t.r. Comstock. 341: t.r. Comstock. 343: t.r. Comstock. 344: b.c.l., b.l. courtesy of Sonor Instruments, a division of Hohner, HSS. 345: t.l., c.l., b.l. courtesy of Sonor Instruments, a division of Hohner, HSS. 346: b.l., c.l. courtesy of Sonor Instruments, a division of Hohner, HSS. 354: t.l. PhotoDisc, Inc. 354-355: bkgd. PhotoDisc, Inc. 356-357: t.l. Image Club Graphics; bkgd. PhotoDisc, Inc. 359: t. Paul Natkin/Getty Images. 360: t.l. PhotoDisc, Inc. 360-361: b.c. PhotoDisc, Inc. 360-361: bkgd. MetaCreations/Kai Power Photos. 361: b. David H. Wells/Corbis; c.r. PhotoDisc, Inc. 362-363: bkgd. PhotoDisc, Inc. 366: bkgd. Corbis. 367: bkgd. Corbis. 368: t.r. PhotoDisc, Inc.; c. PhotoDisc, Inc.; l. MetaCreations/Kai Power Photos. 368-369: bkgd. Quarasan. 370-371: bkgd. t. Image Club Graphics. 372: t.l., t.r. PhotoDisc, Inc. 372-373: c.r., bkgd. PhotoDisc, Inc. 374: t. PhotoDisc, Inc. 374-375: bkgd. PhotoDisc, Inc. 375: b., t. PhotoDisc, Inc. 376-377: bkgd. PhotoDisc, Inc. 379: t.r. David Young-Wolff/PhotoEdit, Inc.; l. Travis Morisse/The Hutchinson News/AP Photo. 380: b.l. PhotoEdit, Inc.; t.c., b. PhotoDisc, Inc. 383: t.l. Flip Schulke/Corbis. 384-385: bkgd. MetaCreations/Kai Power Photos. 386: t.r. PhotoDisc, Inc.; t.l. Image Club Graphics. 386-387: bkgd. MetaCreations/Kai Power Photos. 388: t.l. Library of Congress, LC-USZ62-13016. 388-389: bkgd. Image Club Graphics; bkgd. PhotoDisc, Inc. 389: t.r. Wildside Press; b. Digital Stock Corp. 390: t.r., t.l. PhotoDisc, Inc. 390-391: t. MetaCreations/Kai Power Photos; c.r., b.c. PhotoDisc, Inc.; bkgd. Corbis. 391: b.l. PhotoDisc, Inc.; t. MetaCreations/Kai Power Photos; b.c.r., b.r. PhotoDisc, Inc. 392-393: bkgd. Corbis. 394: t.l., b.l. PhotoDisc, Inc.; b. Corbis. 394-395: t.c., b.c. PhotoDisc, Inc. 395: b.r. Corbis. 397: b. Joe Sohm/The Image Works. 399: t.l., b.r. PhotoDisc, Inc.; b.l. PhotoDisc Blue/Getty Images. 400: c.l., c.r. PhotoDisc, Inc.; b. Jules Frazier/PhotoDisc Green/Getty Images. 401: t.l., b. PhotoDisc, Inc. 402: t.l. PhotoDisc, Inc. 403: t.l.l., t.r. PhotoDisc, Inc. 404: b.r., t. PhotoDisc, Inc.

All attempts have been made to provide complete and correct credits by the time of publication.

410

Classified Index

CHORAL SONGS

FOLK AND TRADITIONAL

African

African American

American *see also* African American; Native American; Puerto Rican

Alphabetical Index

Global Voices

Interviews

INDEX OF SONGS AND SPEECH PIECES

Pronunciation Key

Simplified International Phonetic Alphabet

VOWELS

ɑ	f<u>a</u>ther	o	<u>o</u>bey	æ	c<u>a</u>t	ɔ	p<u>a</u>w
e	ch<u>a</u>otic	u	m<u>oo</u>n	ɛ	p<u>e</u>t	ʊ	p<u>u</u>t
i	b<u>ee</u>	ʌ	<u>u</u>p	ɩ	<u>i</u>t	ə	<u>a</u>go

SPECIAL SOUNDS

β   say *b* without touching lips together; *Spanish* nue<u>v</u>e, ha<u>b</u>a

ç   <u>h</u>ue; *German* i<u>ch</u>

ð   <u>th</u>e; *Spanish* to<u>d</u>o

ŋ̩   sound <u>n</u> as individual syllable

ö   form [o] with lips and say [e]; *French* ad<u>ieu</u>, *German* sch<u>ö</u>n

œ   form [ɔ] with lips and say [ɛ] *French* c<u>oeu</u>r, *German* pl<u>ö</u>tzlich

ɾ   flipped r; bu<u>tt</u>er

r̄   rolled r; *Spanish* pe<u>rr</u>o

ɫ   click tongue on the ridge behind teeth; *Zulu* <u>ngc</u>wele

ü   form [u] with lips and say [i]; *French* t<u>u</u>, *German* gr<u>ü</u>n

ʊ̈   form [ʊ] with lips and say [ɩ]

x   blow strong current of air with back of tongue up; *German* Ba<u>ch</u>, *Hebrew* <u>H</u>anukkah, *Spanish* ba<u>j</u>o

ʒ   plea<u>s</u>ure

ʼ   glottal stop, as in the exclamation "uh, oh!" [ʌ̓ ŏ]

~   nasalized vowel, such as *French* b<u>on</u> [bõ]

¬   end consonants *k*, *p*, and *t* without puff of air, such as s<u>k</u>y (no puff of air after *k*), as opposed to *k*ite (puff of air after *k*)

OTHER CONSONANTS PRONOUNCED SIMILAR TO ENGLISH

ch	<u>ch</u>eese	ny	o<u>n</u>ion; *Spanish* ni<u>ñ</u>o
g	<u>g</u>o	sh	<u>sh</u>ine
ng	si<u>ng</u>	ts	boa<u>ts</u>